SAFE AND SAVVY INVESTING
FOR THE MIDDLE-INCOME MIDDLE-AGER

Safe and Savvy

Investing

for the

Middle-Income

Middle-Ager

Daniel A. McGowan

Scott, Foresman and Company

Glenview, Illinois   London

ISBN 0-673-24930-1

Copyright © 1990 Daniel A. McGowan.
All Rights Reserved.
Printed in the United States of America.

Library of Congress Cataloging-in-Publication Data
McGowan, Daniel A.
     Safe and savvy investing for the middle-income middle-ager / by
Daniel A. McGowan.
          p.   cm.
     Bibliography: p.
     Includes index.
     ISBN 0-673-24930-1
     1. Finance, Personal. 2. Investments. 3. Portfolio management.
I. Title.
HG179.M383   1989
332.6'78—dc20   89-6413
                                                                          CIP

1 2 3 4 5 6 MPC 94 93 92 91 90 89

Scott, Foresman professional books are available
for bulk sales at quantity discounts. For
information, please contact Marketing Manager,
Professional Books Group, Scott, Foresman and Company,
1900 East Lake Avenue, Glenview, IL 60025.

To Monika, Margit, and Kristina,
and to the students
at Hobart and William Smith Colleges

PREFACE

Most personal finance books devote several chapters to such topics as the importance of financial planning, the construction of a monthly income and expense statement, the construction of a balance sheet, the use and misuse of charge cards, the need for insurance, the reasons for saving, the way Social Security may affect retirement planning, and the essentials of wills, estates, trusts, and death taxes. The focus of this book is different, in part, because it is addressed to middle-income, middle-aged people who are already familiar with these areas of personal finance. Such people already know the importance of financial planning. They could construct both income and wealth statements, although, like most people, they do not actually take the time to do so. They do not need a lecture on credit cards; they are already sensitive to annual percentage rates and finance charges associated with credit cards and other debts.

Middle-income middle-agers know how to save by simply abstaining from current consumption or by deliberately setting aside a portion of current income for savings and then spending only what remains of current income. They are not young people learning for the first time about life insurance, health insurance, automobile insurance, and home-owners' insurance. They know the basics about Social Security and retirement and estate planning. And when they need more specific information, they go to books that deal with these topics in greater depth.

The purpose of this book is to examine alternative types of savings and investments that may be attractive to middle-income, middle-wealth people who have defined financial goals and levels of risk they are willing to take to achieve them. It is a very practical, unbiased treatment of a broad range of financial savings and investments. It is not a "get-rich-quick" book like many of those advertised on late-night television. There are no revelations or secret formulas for financial success. However, the reader will discover new approaches to making his or her personal wealth grow at realistic, achievable rates of return.

This book assumes that its readers may be already knowledgeable in particular areas of investment. However, it does not address topics in street talk (Wall Street, that is) or in correlation coefficients, beta coefficients, analyses of variance, or other complicated terms that readers are not likely to be able to use. Instead, the book describes a broad range of ways to make personal wealth grow. It can be used by people with small investment portfolios (e.g., $10,000), medium ones (e.g., $50,000) and large ones (e.g., $500,000).

This book will be useful to conservative investors who might favor blue chip stocks, U.S. Treasury bonds, and large, established mutual funds. It is also useful for more aggressive investors who typically aim for rates of return over 20 percent and who are ready to take higher risks for the promise of getting higher returns. Both types of investors are advised to look at their entire portfolios and not to narrow their attention to a couple of investments while ignoring other investments promising the same returns with lower risk.

A basic characteristic of our investments is simplicity and ease. To own and manage a nightclub might be an excellent investment for a 30-year-old person, particularly one who enjoys the contemporary music scene. But it is not likely to be as attractive for an older investor who might lack such "music appreciation" and who would likely find it more burdensome, say, to count the night's take at 4 o'clock in the morning. Similarly, trading options and futures contracts or making other very speculative investments might be fine for a younger, high-risk investor who is connected to the market and has plenty of years to correct mistakes in judgment. For people who find that wild gyrations in an investment's value cause anxiety and tension, however, there are many more stable alternatives. It is not that risky investments are ignored in this book, but rather that the focus is on alternatives that are more likely to be consistent with the goals and propensity for risk of a middle-ager.

The book begins with a basic discussion of the fundamentals of saving and investment. *Do not skip this chapter.* It is very important because it builds the framework for the rest of the book. It also explains the basic approach of putting money into an investment, letting it "cook" along for a certain length of time, and comparing what you get out of it with the initial investment to determine an annual rate of return. This is an introduction, a very simple one, but unless it is well understood, later discussions and computations will be more difficult. Several practice exercises are included to allow the reader to feel more comfortable with a simple hand-held calculator.

The second chapter looks at alternate places to keep savings. The emphasis is on safe places to store money where you can quickly and easily get it back (liquidity) and where at the same time you can earn some interest to compensate for having left it somewhere other than in your checking account. Banks, other savings institutions, and money-market deposits are described and compared.

Chapters 3 to 7 cover the main forms of financial and real investments. (By *real investments* economists mean additions to one's stock of goods used to produce other goods. Real investments include tangible capital, such as calculators, tools, and machinery, and intangible capital, such as education and technical training.) Chapter 3 examines stocks, how to buy and sell them, and some of the basic terminology used in the stock market. Chapter 4 covers bonds and other fixed-income securities, with particular emphasis on mortgages. Chapter 5 deals with mutual funds, options, commodity futures contracts, index futures contracts, and options on futures contracts.

Chapter 6 is rather unique because it examines the savings/investment portion of life insurance and separates it from the pure insurance portion. Chapter 7 looks at the advantages and disadvantages of real estate as an investment.

The last chapter describes how an investment portfolio can be set up and monitored. The individual's portfolio is essentially treated as a mutual fund, so that net asset values can be compared for different points in time and rates of return can be computed for aggregate personal wealth as well as for individual assets. The rules for portfolio monitoring are clearly described, and a sample portfolio is tracked to show the impacts of buying and selling, share dividends and interest, and cash dividends taken out of the portfolio.

CONTENTS

1

FUNDAMENTALS OF SAVING AND FINANCIAL INVESTMENT

Many people find it difficult to distinguish personal saving from personal investment. While most agree that depositing money in a passbook bank account is an act of saving, many say that the purchase of a certificate of deposit (CD) at the same bank is a form of investment. If Mr. Jones takes $5000 and buys CDs, they say he invested in CDs. On the other hand, if Mr. Jones buys $5000 worth of U.S. Savings Bonds, which mature in 10 years, some of these same people might consider this an act of saving. (The advertisement for Savings Bonds adds to the confusion by saying, "Take stock in America. Invest in U.S. Savings Bonds.") At the other end of the saving-investment spectrum, most people treat the purchase of stocks and corporate bonds as personal financial investments, not as saving. The same is true for purchases of mutual funds, options, commodity futures, gold, or antiques; they are all generally regarded as investments.

What distinguishes saving from investment? Or what distinguishes savings (what is saved) from investments (what is invested)? We shall begin by answering these questions. Then we shall turn our attention to basic investment strategies.

SAVINGS VS. INVESTMENTS

Savings are *liquid* assets temporarily stored before being converted into money that will later be used to purchase consumption goods, real investments (such as houses, automobiles used for business, tools, machinery, etc.), and financial investments (such as stocks and bonds). The emphasis is on *liquidity*: the ease with which the asset can be converted to money. A checking account is very, very liquid; it is usually accepted as money, and it can often be converted to cash with the stroke of a pen. A savings account is also very liquid but may require a trip to the bank to convert it to cash. On the other hand, a CD is less liquid, since 30 days' notice is sometimes required before it can be cashed prior to maturity, and even then there is a penalty equal to at least a loss of 3 months' interest. A stock is also not very liquid and usually requires several days to be sold or converted to money. Real estate is even less liquid, or more illiquid, and may take months to sell and be converted to money.

The purpose of holding savings is to *conserve personal wealth* and to make it available for transformation or change into other assets. The purpose of financial investments, on the other hand, is to *expand personal wealth,* not just to conserve it.

Think about checking accounts, NOW accounts, savings and loan association shares, credit union shares, and ordinary passbook accounts. They are all short-term storehouses for liquid personal wealth. So are shares in money market mutual funds, which will be discussed in detail in Chapter 2. To a lesser extent, certificates of deposit and savings bonds are also held primarily to conserve personal wealth until it is needed for something else. Although most of these assets earn interest, this is not their principal attraction. They are held for safety, liquidity, and as storehouses of personal wealth.

Now think about stocks, bonds, real estate held for speculation, diamonds, gold, rare stamps, and works of art. These are forms of *financial investments*. Financial investments are different from *real investments,* which are increases in the quantity or quality of capital, meaning goods used to produce other goods. The purchase of a spark plug wrench is a real investment; it is a tangible piece of capital used to produce another good, e.g., a smoother-running car. Real investments also can be intangible, such as a college or technical-school education. On the other hand, financial investments are assets, such as stocks, bonds, and diamonds, that are not used *directly* to produce anything. (Of course, we are not talking about industrial diamonds used for cutting steel or gold used for dental work.) Financial assets are valued because they are expected to yield interest or dividends and/or because they are expected to appreciate in value. In either case, the primary purpose of holding any kind of financial investment is to increase the size of personal wealth, not just to store it.

Let's explore some of the reasons why people choose to hold a portion of their wealth in easily accessible, liquid forms.

MOTIVES FOR HOLDING LIQUID ASSETS

Economic theory teaches that there are four basic motives for holding savings or any liquid asset. It is wise to examine these carefully in the abstract so that they may be related to the wide range of specific personal financial assets.

The *transactions motive* for holding liquid assets lies in the expectation that these assets can be easily exchanged for other goods and services. Cash, checking accounts, NOW accounts, and money market mutual funds with check-writing privileges are examples of assets held primarily for transactions purposes. (These will all be discussed in detail in Chapter 2.) You hold a portion of your wealth in the form of these assets because such assets can serve as mediums for exchange in making desired transactions.

The *precautionary motive* for holding liquid assets lies in the expectation that they can be easily used in case of an emergency or to buy something in a hurry. All the assets mentioned in the preceding paragraph satisfy the precautionary motive, but so do savings accounts, U.S. Savings Bonds, Treasury bills, savings and loan shares, and other assets that can easily be converted into money. The precautionary motive is based on the need for readily available funds in case of an emergency or to take advantage of an opportunity that would be lost if you had to wait to convert other assets into money. Your home may be quite valuable, but it is likely to be illiquid and of limited use in case you suddenly need a couple of hundred dollars in cash.[1]

The *finance motive* for holding liquid assets lies in the hope that these assets can be temporarily stored until their size is large enough to buy a particular item. For example, wealth may be held in the form of a savings account in the hope that it can be added to and will grow to sufficient size to buy a new car.

Finally, the *speculative motive* for holding liquid assets lies in the hope that these assets may preserve wealth better than alternative assets. When the market values of stocks, bonds, and real estate are falling, you may choose to hold liquid assets such as cash and checking accounts in order to maintain—if not increase—your personal wealth. Liquid assets such as savings deposits and money market mutual fund shares are made even more attractive by the interest they pay.

The principal reason for holding illiquid assets, such as stocks and bonds, and even more illiquid assets, such as real estate and diamonds, is that they promise higher returns to compensate for higher risk and for being less liquid.

EXPECTED RATE OF RETURN

The primary motive for holding most financial investments lies in their expected rates of return. Expected returns need not be measured exclusively in monetary terms, however. Indeed, investment returns are often nonmonetary in nature. An obvious example is investment in paintings and other works of art that can provide their owners with continued returns of aesthetic pleasure. Another example is investment in gold bullion that may provide its holders with psychological security far greater than could any other asset, including those expected to appreciate more rapidly in value. The same is true for people who derive satisfaction from owning a piece of land even when the monetary returns from that land in the form of rents and appreciation in market value are relatively small. However, since nonmonetary returns are difficult, if not impossible, to quantify, we shall omit them from the following discussion of the expected returns on an investment. Instead, we shall concentrate on an investment's expected inflow and outflow of monetary returns over time.

Monetary returns may flow from an investment in the form of dividends, interest, rents, or other payments. With stocks, returns are likely to come in the form of the dividends the corporation chooses to pay. With bonds, returns come in the form of a specific amount of interest paid each month, each quarter, or whenever. There are also expected returns associated with such investments as land and capital equipment. For real estate, returns may come in the form of rents as specified in a lease or other financial agreement. The same is true for an investment in a piece of real capital, such as a truck, from which returns may come in the form of rental fees. (If you own and operate the truck, the returns might be in the form of implicit rents for the services the vehicle provides.)

The final return on any investment comes when it is sold. This final return is the net sale price, i.e., the sale price minus broker's fees and other transactions costs.

In the case of a real investment, such as a tool or an appliance, this final return is its scrap value.

MEASURING RATES OF RETURN

To find the rate of return r on any particular investment, it is necessary to know the following pieces of information:

1. The dollar value of the initial investment—call it *IN* for what you put in.
2. The number of years an investment is held—call it t for the length of time.
3. The dollar value of all returns—call it *OUT* for what you get out.

Do not worry about taxes, inflation, and other complications for the moment. The annual rate of return is then found by solving the following equation for r:

$$IN\,(1 + r)^t = OUT$$

We can read this equation for a 1-year investment ($t = 1$) as "what you put in times (1 plus the annual rate of return) equals what you get out after 1 year." For a 2-year investment ($t = 2$), it would read "what you put in times (1 plus the annual rate of return) times (1 plus the annual rate of return) equals what you get out after 2 years" or "what you put in times (1 plus the annual rate of return) squared equals what you get out after 2 years." And for a 3-year investment ($t = 3$), it would read "what you put in times (1 plus the annual rate of return) raised to the third power equals what you would get out after 3 years."

Another way of looking at the formula is that you, the investor, take *IN* dollars, put it in the investment oven, let it "cook" for *t* years, and record what comes *OUT.* No matter how complicated the investment, this approach to finding the rate of return is always the same. Let's consider a few simple examples.

If you take $10,000 and put it in an investment, let it cook along for 1 year, and then sell it for $15,000, your rate of return would be computed as follows:

Since $IN = \$10,000$

$$t = 1 \text{ year}$$

$$OUT = \$15,000$$

Then $10,000(1 + r)^1 = 15,000$

and

$$r = 0.5, \text{ or } 50 \text{ percent per year}$$

If instead your investment had been $8000 and you held it 1 year and then sold it for $9000, the formula would be

$$8000(1 + r)^1 = 9000$$

and

$$r = 0.125, \text{ or } 12.5 \text{ percent per year}$$

If your investment was not made for exactly 1 year, you will need a calculator to solve for *r*, the annual rate of return. Moreover, your calculator must have a y^x key so that you can square ($t = 2$), cube ($t = 3$), or raise any number to any power. Only a few years ago such calculators were not available, and more complex methods were required to solve exponential equations.

Looking at our first example, if it had taken 4 years for your $10,000 investment to grow to $15,000, then our equation would have been

$$10,000(1 + r)^4 = 15,000$$

To solve for r, first divide both sides by 10,000:

$$(1 + r)^4 = \frac{15,000}{10,000} = 1.5$$

Next, get rid of the exponent, 4, on the left-hand side by raising both sides to the ¼ or 0.25 power:

¶ Put 1.5 on your calculator.
¶ Hit the y^x key.
¶ Hit 0.25.
¶ Hit =.

And you have the number 1.1066819. Therefore,

$$1 + r = 1.1066819$$

and

$$r = 0.1066819, \text{ or 10.67 percent per year.}$$

This means that over the 4 years you held this investment, it grew at a compound annual rate of return of 10.67 percent.

Try the same exercise for the $8000 investment, now held for 4 years to become $9000. You will see that its annual rate of return drops to 2.99 percent per year.

The costs of buying and selling investments, i.e., transactions costs, must be considered when computing rates of return. In our first example, suppose that it cost $500 in legal fees to buy a $10,000 piece of land and $2000 in broker fees to sell it. Our formula would have to be modified, with the $500 added to the initial investment (IN) and the $2000 subtracted from the proceeds (OUT). So,

$$(10,000 + 500)(1 + r)^4 = 15,000 - 2000$$

$$(1 + r) = (13,000/10,500)^{0.25}$$

and

$$r = 5.48 \text{ percent per year}$$

Transactions costs have drastically lowered a 10.67 percent investment to render it a 5.48 percent investment.

The rates of return will be negative if the proceeds (OUT) do not exceed the initial investment (IN)—in other words, if a loss occurs. Examples showing negative rates will be introduced in later chapters. We also shall discuss ways of dealing with periodic income and expenses (other than transactions costs) associated with particular investments. For now, however, rate of return is simply calculated from the formula

$$IN(1 + r)^t = OUT$$

so that
$$r = \left(\frac{OUT}{IN}\right)^{1/t} - 1$$

LIQUIDITY, ILLIQUIDITY, AND TRANSACTIONS COSTS

Associated with every asset held for saving or for investment are three costs that should be compared with the asset's benefits. These involve liquidity, illiquidity, and transactions.

Liquidity cost refers to the interest, dividends, or other returns that are given up (foregone) so personal wealth can be held in a liquid form. It is simply the opportunity cost of being liquid. If a $1000 government bond pays 10 percent interest and you decide to hold $1000 in cash instead of such a bond, the cost of your being liquid is 10 percent, or $100 per year. Liquidity cost is the same as the *opportunity cost* of holding wealth in a liquid form instead of an illiquid form paying a higher yield.

Illiquidity cost is the opportunity cost of being illiquid. If you hold your wealth in cash, there is obviously no illiquidity cost, since cash is perfectly liquid. If you hold wealth in other forms, however, such as stocks and bonds, there might be opportunities that you would have to forgo simply because you could not sell these assets and get into the new opportunities fast enough. There is an even greater illiquidity cost associated with wealth held in the form of real estate or diamonds; here it might easily take months to sell your land or your gems and make the funds available for new investments with higher rates of return.

Transactions cost is the cost to get out of or into an asset. With stocks, there is usually a 3 to 5 percent broker's fee to either buy or sell. For real estate, there are brokers' fees, lawyers' fees, title searches, mortgage fees, and other costs that can easily add up to 10 percent of the average purchase price and subsequent sale price. The transactions costs for art, antiques, and collectibles are even higher, because you are likely to buy at retail and to have to sell at wholesale or below. For example, if you buy an antique chest of drawers for $1000, it is improbable that you could immediately resell it for more than $800. Dealers, who are easy to find, pay at least 20 percent below retail, and you are likely to incur high costs in terms of advertisements and time if you try to search for other people to buy from you at near retail prices.

A good understanding of liquidity, illiquidity, and transactions costs helps in analyzing the motives for holding assets as savings and as investments. It also helps in assessing the benefits of switching among assets—in other words, rearranging your portfolio.

While some investments are held for aesthetic or psychological motives, most investments are desired primarily for their expected rates of return. Nevertheless, it is not enough to rank investments according to their expected rates of return and simply choose those with the highest numbers. Selection is also premised on another very important factor called *risk*.

RISK AS THE DISPERSION OF POSSIBLE RETURNS

Risk has to do with the variability of possible returns on an investment. It is one thing to compute an expected return; it is something else to look at all the possible returns other than the one you expect. *Risk* is a measure of the spread or dispersion of possible returns that an investment might produce. In the case of a $10,000 real estate investment, there is a chance (albeit a slim one) that the land will appreciate to $110,000 during the next year if, say, oil deposits are discovered on it. On the other hand, if chemical or nuclear pollution is discovered on the land, its value might drop to $2000, resulting in a very large negative rate of return.

Very high positive rates of return and very negative rates of return may have low probabilities of occurring. But the dispersion of these possible returns is a measure of the investment's risk. On a 6 percent savings account, for example, it is most probable that you will earn 6 percent. Of course, it is conceivable that bank error or the timing of deposits and withdrawals could result in anything from a 100 percent loss (if both you and the bank lost all records of your having an account) to an enormous positive gain (if other large deposits were inadvertently and permanently credited to your account). These events are highly unlikely, however. The probability dis-

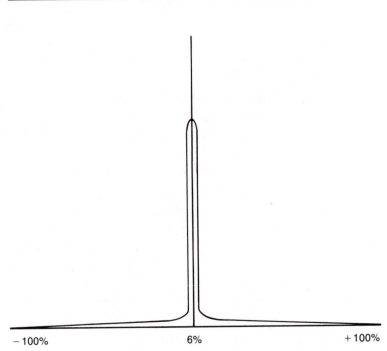

−100%　　　　　　　　　　6%　　　　　　　　　　+100%

FIGURE 1.1　The probability distribution for the return on a 6 percent savings account is very narrow.

tribution for the possible returns on a savings account might look like the curve shown in Figure 1.1. The dispersion of these returns is very narrow, which means the risk for gains and losses deviating from 6 percent is very low.

Holding gold bullion as a financial investment has a considerably higher risk. Gold fluctuates greatly in price. The variance in its price spells greater probabili-

| −100% | −50% | 6% | +50% | +100% |

FIGURE 1.2   The average rate of return on an investment in gold bullion might also be 6 percent, but the risk or dispersion of possible rates of return is much higher.

ties for both significant appreciation and depreciation from the current value of gold compared to what you paid for it. Transactions costs (including assaying charges) and storage charges tend to reduce the benefits of appreciation and magnify the losses of depreciation. The probability distribution for the returns on an investment in gold bullion might look like the curve shown in Figure 1.2. Compared to the probability distribution for returns on a savings account, the dispersion, or variance, for returns on an investment in gold is rather wide; this means the risk for gains *and* for losses is high. If you like to be sure of your rate of return, gold bullion is not the investment for you. It is a speculative investment with great variance in its possible rates of return.

SOURCES OF RISK

The variance, or dispersion, of the possible rates of return on an investment stems primarily from business risk, market risk, and political risk.

Business risk is the variation in the earning power of the company or government backing the financial asset. If bank earnings decline, interest paid on bank securities may decline. The same is true for stocks and bonds, for which dividends and interest may change as a result of changes in the earning power and financial well-being of the issuing companies. A similar case exists for the rents paid on a lease, since the payment of rent is often premised on the earning power of the leaser. In the extreme case of bankruptcy, no rent may be paid to the leaseholder. Business risk directly affects the cash flows that owners of investments can expect to receive.

Market risk is the variation in the market price of an investment resulting from changes in the demand for and/or the supply of that particular kind of investment. Of course, business risk can lead to market risk, since poor earnings may cause reduced demand and hence a fall in the asset's market value. However, market risk is also caused by factors totally unrelated to corporate earnings. For example, the market price of gold can rise or fall independently of the productivity and earnings of gold mining companies. An even better example is the market risk in antiques or rare paintings, which are totally unaffected by business risk because they are no longer produced.

Political risk is the variation in returns caused by

changes in taxes, wage-price controls, subsidy policies, interest-rate ceilings, and other government actions that affect after-tax earnings and hence the investment's market price. An excess profits tax on oil companies, for example, leads to variation in the expected rate of return on oil company stock. Tax credits for insulating a home cause the after-tax returns on this real investment to be greater than expected. A government moratorium on further construction in an area declared to be a "green belt" or an "area forever wild" causes prices of investments in potentially developable land to fall precipitously, while it enhances the returns from existing developments by closing off new competition.

Business, market, and political risk can affect the variance in the possible returns on an initial investment of, say, $10,000. But the variance (and hence the risk) is magnified if the $10,000 is used as a down payment on a $100,000 investment, the balance of which is financed by borrowing. It is one thing to buy a piece of land for $10,000 and expect to reap net rents and appreciation. (*Net rents* are the gross rental receipts minus taxes, insurance, and maintenance expenses.) It is much riskier, but also potentially more profitable, to use the $10,000 as down payment on a $100,000 piece of land and reap its net rents and appreciation. This source of risk is known as *risk generated by leverage*.

LEVERAGE
Leverage is simply the ratio of debt to equity; it is how much you owe relative to how much you own (see Table

**Table 1.1   Greater Leverage Produces Greater
Returns and Greater Losses**

With 90 Percent Leverage	With No Leverage

Capital Gain

$10,000 down payment	$100,000 total payment
$10,000 (gross) capital gain	$10,000 (gross) capital gain
$\dfrac{10{,}000}{10{,}000} = 100\%$ rate of return	$\dfrac{10{,}000}{100{,}000} = 10\%$ rate of return

Capital Loss

$10,000 down payment	$100,000 down payment
$10,000 (gross) capital loss	$10,000 (gross) capital loss
$\dfrac{-10{,}000}{10{,}000} = \begin{array}{l}-100\% \text{ rate of} \\ \text{return, or } 100\% \\ \text{loss}\end{array}$	$\dfrac{-10{,}000}{100{,}000} = \begin{array}{l}-10\% \text{ rate of} \\ \text{return, or } 10\% \\ \text{loss}\end{array}$

1.1). If you buy a $100,000 property with a $10,000 down payment, your leverage is 90 percent; that is, debt divided by equity, or $90,000 divided by $100,000, which equals 90 percent. Similarly, if you buy $8000 worth of stocks with $6000 of your own money and $2000 borrowed from the stockbroker, your leverage would be 25 percent: $2000 divided by $8000 equals 25 percent.

The greater your leverage, the greater is the chance for a high rate of return on your original investment. Take an extreme example in which you buy a house for $10,000 down with a $90,000 mortgage. Assume that the house appreciates to $110,000 after 1 year and that you sell it. If we ignore the transfer costs (such as lawyers' fees, mortgage fees, etc.) of buying and selling and ignore the interest paid on the mortgage, taxes, and other costs, then your gross rate of return on the $10,000 invested would be

$$10,000(1 + r)^1 = 110,000 - 90,000$$

$$(1 + r) = \frac{20,000}{10,000} = 2$$

$$r = 1, \text{ or } 100 \text{ percent per year}$$

Had you bought the house outright for $100,000 in cash, your overall rate of return would have been

$$100,000(1 + r)^1 = 110,000$$

$$(1 + r) = \frac{110,000}{100,000} = 1.1$$

$$r = 0.10, \text{ or } 10 \text{ percent per year}$$

Leverage increases the dispersion of possible rates of return on an investment. The higher the leverage, the greater is the variance in the distribution of expected rates of return; i.e., the greater is the risk.

It should not be assumed, however, that higher leverage (and hence higher risk) is always beneficial. Rates of return can be negative (representing losses) as well as positive. Had you sold the house for $90,000, 90 percent leverage would have meant a 100 percent loss on your $10,000 investment. (Again, we are neglecting rents, taxes, and interest on the borrowed funds.)

$$10,000(1 + r)^1 = 90,000 - 90,000$$

$$(1 + r) = \frac{0}{90,000} = 0$$

$$r = -1, \text{ or } -100 \text{ percent per year}$$

If you had purchased the house for $100,000 in cash, your loss would only have been 10 percent:

$$100,000(1 + r)^1 = 90,000$$

$$(1 + r) = \frac{90,000}{100,000} = 0.9$$

$$r = -0.1, \text{ or } -10 \text{ percent per year}$$

We shall see the effects of leveraging again in Chapter 3 when we examine borrowing to buy stocks, i.e., buying stocks on the margin. We also shall see it again in Chapter 5 in the markets for options and commodity futures.

At this point, we shift gears. We shall move away from the underlying motives for holding savings and investments and look instead at some of the actual techniques of choosing among the thousands of savings and investment alternatives offered in the market.

PORTFOLIO SELECTION

It is not easy to select financial investments that consistently outperform the market or earn a better than average rate of return. The very definition of average rate of return suggests that about half of all investments do not outperform the market. All investors would like to buy low, earn lots of dividends, interest, or other returns, and sell when the price is high. In fact, however, many follow P. T. Barnum's law suggesting that the sucker born every minute will grow up, invest at high prices, earn nothing, and sell just when the market hits its lowest point.

Hundreds of books and articles have been written on strategies for developing investment portfolios and formulas for outguessing—and hence outperforming—the market. The theories range from the fatalistic (no strategy is the best strategy) to the impossible (a strategy "guaranteed" to yield 1000 percent and more each year). Here are some of the popular approaches taken by individual investors.

Professional Advice

Perhaps the easiest approach—although not necessarily the most economical—is to purchase your strategy from professional investment advisors. Any reputable stock brokerage firm can provide current information on most stocks, bonds, mutual funds, stock options, commodity options, and other financial investments. Usually this information is given without charge; it is paid for by commissions earned by the company when you and other investors buy and sell securities.

Many consumerists feel that you get better advice from an investment advisor or financial counselor who charges a fee for this service but who receives no commission on investments that you end up purchasing. They regard brokers as simply salespeople who usually will not recommend any investment that they do not sell and hence on which they will not make a commission. This is a valid criticism of brokers. On the other hand, there are many very knowledgeable and forthright brokers, and there is no guarantee of quality advice from a financial counselor no matter how much he or she charges.

A good full-service broker or an investment advisor can help you to examine a number of alternative investments that promise to meet your goals. In frequent discussions with such a person you will come to decide how much risk you can and are willing to assume. Both you and the advisor get a feel for your need for current income and your financial and psychological ability to buy investments whose values may vary greatly over time.

Brokers can provide good information on investments that are monitored by their firms' research departments. Company reports, analysts' opinions, and factors that are likely to affect the value of a particular investment (factors such as changes in interest rates, changes in prices, changes in weather, and changes in other conditions that affect the industry and hence the firm) are readily available to them and, through them, to you. For companies which they monitor, brokers can tell you whether a stock looks good based on its earnings, its price-to-earnings ratio, its asset-to-liability ratio, and other measures of corporate strength. You could probably get the same information on your own, but your research would involve considerable time and your data would not likely be as up-to-date.

If you have a large investment portfolio—at least $25,000 to $50,000—a broker can usually set up an account and manage everything for you. Buying and selling can be done subject to your discretion (i.e., you act on suggestions made by the broker), or it can be done at the broker's discretion, assuming, of course, that you have authorized him or her to trade in your name. Once a month you will receive a statement of the transactions made, interest earned, dividends received, commissions charged, and the current balance in your account.

Brokers provide service as well as act as salespeople. With your permission, they may keep your stock certificates in their company's name, which has the advantage of allowing the stock to be sold immediately without having to obtain your signature. This is particularly advantageous if you want to sell but are away from home or find it inconvenient to dig out the securities, sign them, and take them to the broker. Brokers pay interest on cash balances left in your account, and the interest rate on these balances is usually greater than the passbook rate paid at banks.

Brokers also are willing to lend their clients money to buy securities. Such purchases are said to be made *at the margin*. Margin requirements are set by the Federal Reserve Board (Regulation T) and specify what portion of security purchases can be lent by brokers. For example, brokers can only finance 50 percent of a stock transaction. Naturally, brokers earn interest as well as commissions on sales made at the margin. However, the ability to borrow quickly and easily provides you with easy leverage and the chance for higher returns on your investment.

The problem with relying on professional advice is that it costs money. (More will be said on broker charges in Chapter 3.) Advice and portfolio management are not free goods. In addition, the advice is limited to the investments usually handled by the stockbroker. You are not likely to get advice or data comparing returns in the stock market with expected returns on investing in local real estate, antiques, or a host of other alternatives that might be better for you. Moreover, brokers generally try to persuade you to buy and build a portfolio with them. They give far more recommendations to buy than recommendations to sell, even when they are not deliberately "churning their accounts" (buying and selling stocks) to generate new commissions.

The "professional wisdom" of investment advisers is given a sobering—if not cynical—dousing with cold water by those investors who adhere to the next strategy, known as the *random walk*.

The Random Walk

Some investors believe that it is not possible to enter an active market and deliberately buy investments yielding above-average returns. They argue that other investors—especially those with genuine inside information—will already have sensed a particular investment's potential and will have bid up its market price accordingly. On the other side of the spectrum, the demand will fall for investments that promise neither good annual returns nor competitive rates of appreciation. The prices of these investments will fall, resulting in a potentially higher overall yield or rate of return, which will again approach the market average.

This theory is known as the *random-walk hypothesis,* also known as the *efficient-market theory.* It suggests that all investment yields will tend toward the mean or average rate of return. Low and high yields will occur, but they cannot be predicted. Anything predictable will be discounted or adjusted in the market price of the investment. As a result, an investor, even a so-called professional, is no more likely to select a portfolio that will outperform the market than if he or she chose investments by randomly throwing darts at the stock listings in the *Wall Street Journal.*

Proponents of the random-walk theory claim that professional investors show no better returns on their investments in the long run than the overall averages for the types of investments involved. In other words, random selection gives the same rate of return over the long run as will careful, professional selection. As evidence, they cite studies that compared the performance of A-plus stock investments with the average of all stocks listed on the New York Stock Exchange over a 10-year period. These studies found that over half the stocks rated A-plus did not do as well as the New York Stock Exchange average (*Changing Times,* March 1976, pp. 7–10). A more recent study was even more damaging to the supposed benefits of professional advice and management. Of 40 investment newsletters, only three provided advice, which would have led to a rate of return equal to or exceeding the 15.5 percent compound annual growth rate of the Standard & Poor's 500 stock index over the 5-year period ending in 1988 (*Wall Street Journal,* June 7, 1988, p. 33).

In some ways, the random-walk theory is a cop-out. It says that there is no profit (at least not in the long run) from studying and carefully choosing investments; it condones, or rationalizes, simply picking an investment, any investment listed, for example, on the New York Stock Exchange, and hoping that it will yield and appreciate at or above the average. To the extent that it leaves an investor with a fatalistic attitude in which there is no control over one's own life, it is demeaning. On the other hand, the random-walk theory is also sobering for someone trying to evaluate the benefits of buying investment and financial management services. If the professional managers cannot do better than you can on your own, why bother to pay for their services? (One answer, of course, is that you may find it worthwhile to pay for the bookkeeping, cash management, and lending services the brokers provide.)

The biggest problem with the random-walk theory is it assumes that all investors have the same access to market information, that they read and absorb it, and that they adjust their portfolios accordingly. This is simply not the case. Many investors are extremely lackadaisical about their present holdings; they are seemingly unconcerned about current changes, including those which may have an impact on the earnings and potential appreciation of their investments. They rationalize this behavior by claiming to be "in it for the long run" or by pointing to the high cost of their time, energy, and money "to stay on top of the market."

Other investors are stubbornly irrational. They hold a losing stock for years, hoping it will again rise to the price they paid for it, at which point they plan to immediately dump it. In the meantime, they receive low earnings and forego the opportunity to reinvest the money elsewhere in order to avoid taking a capital loss. This attitude is quite widespread among unsophisticated and usually small investors.

The majority of investors, however, even the wise ones, are unable to process all the information necessary to discount investments, so their prices are bid up or down causing the yields to shift toward the overall average yield. Most experts believe that "mining" investment data, i.e., picking away at positive and negative indicators and shoveling through the hype generated by brokers, dealers, and journalists trying to fill their weekly financial columns, can still be very profitable in the search for above-average returns. In other words, they believe that it is possible to consistently pick investments that are winners.

Picking Winners

If picking investments that outperform the market were easy, lots of individuals and institutions would demand these investments. They would bid their prices up and thereby reduce the potential for capital gains. However, consistently picking winners is difficult. It requires considerable study, a feel for the market, and a bit of luck.

One indicator commonly used in the stock market is the price-to-earnings (*P/E*) ratio. A low *P/E* ratio indicates that the company has high earnings per share relative to the current price at which a share is selling in the market. This suggests that the market has undervalued this company's stock and that it is a good buy at its current low price.[2]

A more important consideration is the trend in earnings per share. Are these earnings expected to rise, showing strength and growth of the company? Are inventories falling relative to current production, indicating the potential for the company to expand and increase total earnings? Were earnings affected by the sale of corporate assets, by the appreciation of liquid assets held abroad, or for any other reason than expanded output and the potential for being a profitable business?

A second, closely associated indicator is the price-to-dividend (*P/D*) ratio. Dividends are one portion of earnings; the other two parts are (1) corporate income taxes and (2) retained earnings (earnings neither paid to the government nor to the shareholder). The *P/D* ratio suggests the *payback period,* i.e., the number of years you need to wait before dividends received will be equal to the price you paid for the stock. Presumably, the lower the *P/D* ratio, the better the investment. But like the *P/E* ratio, the *P/D* ratio ignores the potential for stock prices to rise, i.e., for a capital gain. Moreover, it is important not only to recognize current dividends, but also to assess whether these dividends will be maintained in the future.

For investments with low dividends (growth stocks) and investments with no earnings or dividends (vacant land, gold, diamonds, antique cars, and collectibles), the *P/E* and *P/D* ratios are meaningless. What is important here is how fast prices will rise, i.e., how fast the market value will appreciate.

A third indicator is the amount and kind of assets (relative to the number of shareholders) a company holds and how valuable these assets might become in the future. Like the other indicators, this one can be tricky. For example, in the 1960s, the Penn Central Railroad had a lot of assets relative to its number of stockholders, yet the company steadily went downhill and was a very poor investment.

A portion of liquid assets that a company or mutual fund holds also may be helpful information for picking a winner. In times of rapid growth, holding large amounts of liquid assets (such as certificates of deposit, Treasury bills, etc.) with low interest yields can signify a relatively poor investment. On the other hand, these same liquid-asset holdings are indicators of strength when the stock and bond markets are falling or when liquid assets are available to take advantage of other investment opportunities.

Finally, picking winners among investments requires a feel for where the economy is headed and how it will affect the specific markets you are considering. If the trend is toward vacation homes, perhaps now is the time to buy one or rent one with the option to buy at a fixed price. If the stock market is "peaking," perhaps now is the time to move into bonds, gold, or money market funds. This kind of decision making requires sophistication and self-confidence. It is more difficult because you are taking the bull by the horns (or the bear by the tail) instead of simply following brokers' suggestions. The only consolation is that if you wait until the average person thinks something is a good investment, you have almost always waited too long. By that time, the market prices are already changing, leaving expected returns on the investment mediocre at best. *The key to picking the winners is timing,* i.e., the ability to anticipate emerging trends and to act accordingly.

If picking winners is difficult, and it is if we believe the millions of investors whose "sure bets" have gone sour, avoiding the losers is much easier. Although not a novel approach for sophisticated individuals and institutional investors, loss avoidance is a relatively novel strategy for most people.

Avoiding Losers

A businessperson who is trying to maximize the XYZ Company's profits will charge the same price and sell the same quantity as the businessperson who is trying to minimize the company's losses. Because profits are simply negative losses and losses are negative profits, the maximization of profits is simply the "flip side" or what economists call the dual of the minimization of losses. This might also be true when employing investment strategies; that is, picking winners would be the dual of avoiding losers, *if* only there were perfect and complete information available to the investor. Unfortunately, information is scarce and one-sided.

One of the reasons it is more difficult to pick a winner is that there are so many investments from which to choose. As a result, a huge amount of information needs to be digested before a selection is made. When culling out a loser from a portfolio of investments, attention and information can be focused on a far smaller number of stocks, bonds, or whatever. Consequently, it is easier to spot a loser in a specific portfolio than it is to choose a winner from a much larger number of candidates in the investment "universe."

The second reason why losers are easier to spot than winners lies in the quality of the information gathered. With more time to concentrate on the relatively few issues in a single portfolio (typically no more than ten), each issue can be more closely scrutinized. It is possible to uncover negative information that has not been widely disseminated and hence has not already been digested and discounted by investors at large. As you saw earlier, brokers are generally "bullish" on securities; they want people to buy more often than to sell. As a result, they spread the good news far more than the bad news. As the supply of good news increases, however, it becomes less and less valuable relative to the fewer, lesser known, juicy pieces of bad news.

Every broker wanting to sell XYZ stock will tell you how the company's earnings rose last year, but only a close look at the financial statement would reveal that this was primarily due to a one-time capital gain on a piece of land the company sold. Dealers in collectibles love to tell how a rare copy of the Gutenberg *Bible* (printed in 1499) rose from $1.8 million to $2 million in 2 months. What they do not tell is how very thin the market is for such high-priced collectibles or how the previous owner had bought the *Bible* for $1.8 million, held it for six years, and sold it for exactly the same price, yielding no profit whatsoever.

Bad news is also less plentiful for other investments. Gun dealers are full of stories of how the prices of antique guns have skyrocketed in recent years. Yet they provide no assessment of the impact of gun-control laws on the value of such collections. The same is true for the people who sell diamonds and gold to individual investors wanting tangible assets for safety and appreciation. They are quick to point out sharp rises in prices but reluctant to provide information on reselling these commodities, on broker and appraisal fees, and on the outright diamond and gold frauds that have cost investors thousands of dollars.

Occasionally, a news documentary, such as CBS's *60 Minutes* or ABC's *20/20 News Magazine,* will expose the negative side of certain blatant investment schemes. There is at least one investment research service that specializes in negative critiques of stock investments (*Quality of Earnings Reports,* by Thorton O'Glove and Robert Olstein, The Free Press, 1987). *Consumer Reports, Money, Changing Times,* and a few select newspaper columns also present negative information on certain investments. However, such articles are largely dwarfed by the mass of positive information and unadulterated promotion designed to generate more investment.

The strategy of avoiding losers is much simpler and less time-consuming than trying to pick winners. Some people randomly select investments according to their individual preferences for growth, income, liquidity, and risk. Then they concentrate on these investments and watch them for signs of becoming potential losers. When they spot one or read about one in the few sources of negative information, they get rid of it (divest) and choose another that has shown no serious signs of becoming a loser, at least not yet.

Dollar Cost Averaging

Dollar cost averaging is a strategy for the long-term investor who has neither the time nor the inclination to continually try to outguess the market. It is a proven method best suited for those who like to invest about the same amount of money at regular intervals.

An investor using dollar cost averaging buys $x worth of a particular company's stock (or mutual fund shares, gold, or whatever) every month, every 2 months, or at some other regular interval. When the price is low, the investor gets a larger number of shares for $x; when the price is high, he or she gets a smaller number. Purchases are made irrespective of the price changes. Over the long run, the investor picks up more shares at lower

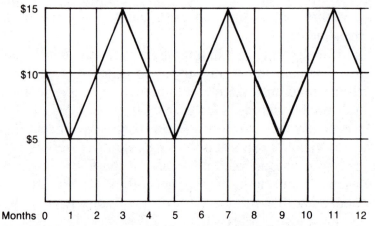

FIGURE 1.3 The prices for a highly volatile investment over 1 year. Such an investment is ideal for employing the dollar cost averaging strategy.

prices than at higher prices, meaning that the average cost of the entire portfolio is less than the average price for the particular investment. To reduce risk, the same strategy can be employed with a number of investments instead of just one.

Dollar cost averaging works best for investments with low transaction costs or no transaction costs at all. It also works better for investments that are highly volatile, i.e., those whose prices or net asset values fluctuate greatly over time. Figure 1.3 shows such a hypothetical volatile investment for a 12-month period; there are three peaks and three troughs among the cyclical fluctuations. An investor who bought $9750 worth of shares initially at $10 per share would end the year with exactly the same amount, i.e., with 975 shares. There would be no dollar gain or loss, since the price in the twelfth month was also $10 per share.

An investor who bought $750 worth of this stock at the beginning of the year and again each month for the next 12 months also would have spent $9750. (There would be thirteen buys at $750 each.) Unlike the first investor, however, this investor would end the year with 1125 shares worth $11,250. If these shares were sold, there would be a gain of $1500, assuming, of course, that there were no transaction costs (see Table 1.2).

No-load mutual funds are well suited for the dollar cost averaging strategy. Not only are transaction costs low (especially compared to stocks and collectibles, such as antiques or art work), but you can invest amounts as small as $25 as often as you like. (There is usually a larger minimum purchase required, e.g., $1000, to open an account with such a mutual fund, however.)

There are many ways to modify the dollar cost averaging strategy. For example, some investors like to increase their dollar purchases when the market price declines and reduce their purchases when it increases. However, such variations reduce the main advantages of the dollar cost averaging approach, namely, simplicity, regularity, and the elimination of frequent judgments as to where the market is headed.

Table 1.2 Shares Purchased with a Monthly Investment Over 1 Year

Month	0	1	2	3	4	5	6	7	8	9	10	11	12	Total
Dollars invested	750	750	750	750	750	750	750	750	750	750	750	750	750	$9750
Shares purchased	75	150	75	50	75	150	75	50	75	150	75	50	75	1125

Switch-Hitting

For those who actively manage their investments and enjoy the challenge of making frequent investment decisions, one of the more popular strategies is known as *switch-hitting*. The strategy is to be in stocks when they are rising, in bonds when they are rising, in commodities when they are rising, in options when they are rising, and to switch into liquid assets when everything else is falling. (This is the old speculative motive for holding liquid assets.) The idea is to run with the "bulls" in whatever market is rising and, when the "bulls" leave, to hide from the "bears" in liquid assets, preferably those paying some interest.

One of the main problems with switching has traditionally been the burden of transactions costs. Whenever a switch is made, there are costs in terms of interest lost on funds made liquid during the switch and in terms of broker's fees and other charges to get in and out of a particular investment. With the introduction of money-market mutual funds and the increasing specialization of other mutual funds in particular kinds of stocks, corporate bonds, tax-exempt bonds, and gold shares and options, transaction costs have been drastically reduced for the individual investor. This is certainly the case for true no-load mutual funds, which charge nothing to buy or redeem their shares. (There is no commission, fee, or "load" to get in or out.) However, it is also true for some loaded funds (those which charge a purchase fee or a redemption fee) that permit cost-free switches into other mutual funds with which they have an agreement. Many funds allow switches to be made by merely placing a (toll-free) telephone call with no broker's fees, load charges, or whatever. Moreover, the ability to write checks on a money market mutual fund and continue to earn interest on the balance until the check is cleared has greatly reduced the earnings lost on funds during the switch.

A second, rather formidable, problem, however, continues to plague the switch-hitter's game. This is timing—in other words, exactly when to make the switch into or out of a risky market. If you think the market for stocks will rise, you may want to get into a fund whose assets are predominantly stocks. If you are wrong, however, you may lose considerably before becoming defensive and switching to a safe money market mutual fund. On the other hand, you might cautiously sit in a money market mutual fund and watch the "bulls" race by.

To improve your timing, you can use all kinds of technical indicators of market trends.[3] However, many analysts are skeptical that any technical strategy can ever be employed to consistently achieve above-average returns over the long run. Even professional managers who employ the switch-hitter strategy often have bad timing. (Remember what we mentioned earlier, that only three out of the forty top-selling investment newsletters did better than the average over the 5-year period ending in 1988.) Fundpack, a mutual fund whose assets consist of shares of other mutual funds, claimed that its "aim was to protect the capital slowly built up during rising markets from being suddenly dissipated in a rapidly declining or bear environment." Yet, in the big market slide of 1978, Fundpack's net asset value fell from a gain of 19.4 percent to a loss of 7 percent for the period from December 31, 1977 to October 20, 1978. This example is not the exception. When it comes to having the best timing needed for switch-hitting, even many of the professionals strike out.

This review of popular investment strategies is by no means comprehensive. There are hundreds of other approaches and schemes. If you are unable to remember any of them, at least remember this rule: *No investment strategy is always successful, and most are successful over some limited periods of time.*

POINTS TO REMEMBER
¶ Savings are liquid assets that are being stored in anticipation of being consumed or invested later. The emphasis is on liquidity and on conserving wealth.

¶ Investments are less liquid (or more illiquid) assets whose primary purpose is to expand personal income and/or personal wealth.

¶ Liquid assets are held for transactions, precautionary, finance, and speculative motives. While less-liquid assets also may be held for the last three reasons, their primary attraction is the rate of return they are expected to yield.

¶ Selecting investments can be simplified by relying on professional advice, but such advice costs money and is often biased in the direction of the assets a particular advisor is currently selling and from which he or she earns commissions.

¶ Selecting can be made randomly in the belief that in an efficient market all rates of return move toward a common mean value.

¶ Two other investment-selection strategies are to try to pick winners and to avoid losers. The latter is often easier, since it involves gathering and analyzing less information.

¶ The technique of dollar cost averaging may be suitable for the long run where regular periodic investments will be made with a general disregard for current market fluctuations.

¶ Trying to outguess current market fluctuations by switch-hitting can be successful, but only if your timing is right and if your switches are not subject to high transactions costs.

2

SECURING AND STORING PERSONAL WEALTH

The first financial asset most people acquire is money. Money flows in from earned and unearned income,[1] and money flows out to meet a variety of fixed and variable expenditures. In the interim, it is often left idle and largely ignored. On the other hand, money can be profitably managed to meet the needs for planned short-term transactions, for planned long-term transactions (to "finance" a particular big-ticket item), for unplanned or precautionary expenditures, and for speculative balances (balances held in the belief that the values of other assets are going to fall). In the last chapter we called these the transactions *finance, precautionary,* and *speculative motives* for holding liquid assets.

In this chapter we are going to look not only at money, but at liquid assets in general. While cash might be held at home, most other liquid assets are held at banks and at nonbanks, such as savings and loan associations, mutual savings banks, and credit unions. Money market mutual funds are sufficiently different from both banks and nonbanks to be in a category by themselves. But all these—banks, nonbanks, and money market mutual funds—are financial intermediaries that individuals can use to manage their liquid assets. In opening our discussion of liquid assets, there is no better place to begin than with some cold, hard cash.

COLD, HARD CASH

In spite of the prediction by some that we are moving toward a cashless society, cold cash is still a very important personal asset. For making transactions, cash is the most liquid asset you can hold. There are things you can do with cash that are difficult or impossible to do with other, less liquid assets. For saving, cash provides security and anonymity like no other asset; in 1988, the average American adult held about $1100 in cash. Those who hold less than this amount are counterbalanced by others holding larger "stashes" of cash. Of course, some of these large cash holders are drug dealers and others engaged in illegal activities, but there are also a large number of people, particularly retired people, who hold, say, $10,000 in cash in safe deposit boxes in banks and in floor safes and secret hiding places around their homes. How much cash you should hold depends on a comparison of its costs and benefits to you.

There are two principal types of costs associated with carrying cash or keeping substantial amounts in your home. The first type of cost includes the risk of theft, loss, or an accident, such as a fire or a flood. These costs can be reduced by taking simple precautionary steps. When making transactions in cash, one obvious safeguard is to carry it in a money belt or conceal it elsewhere on your person. At home, cash can be easily stored in a book or record album. It can be buried in a sealed plastic pipe in the backyard or in the garden. Unless a thief's search is extremely thorough, he or she is not likely to find it there. Moreover, cash so protected will be preserved in all but the most severe fires, floods, or other disasters. (While the outside of a book may be seriously damaged by fire or water, the inside remains suprisingly well preserved.)

The second type of cost of carrying or holding cash is the liquidity cost or the interest foregone had this money been deposited in a bank account instead of being held as cash. Unless very large amounts of cash are held, however, this liquidity cost is rather small. At a 5 percent interest rate, to carry $1100 in cash at all times means "suffering" a liquidity cost of only $55 each year (even less when you consider that taxes would likely be paid on the interest received, bringing after-tax interest to less than $55).

The benefits of holding cash depend on the probability of your needing this most liquid of all assets. An obvious benefit is in making small purchases—sometimes planned, sometimes unplanned—that are more conveniently made in cash or that absolutely must be made in cash. A taxi ride, a hamburger at a fast-food place, a candy bar from a vending machine, a haircut, a box of Band-Aids, and other such purchases almost always require cash. (Of course, there are taxi drivers who accept MasterCard and drugstores that will allow you to charge purchases, but these are still the exceptions.)

A second benefit that cash provides is a sense of security when traveling, especially when going off the beaten track where credit cards and traveler's checks are not readily accepted. In spite of the benefits promised by cash substitutes such as credit cards, debit cards, and traveler's checks, there are many small gas stations, towing services, motels, and restaurants that refuse to take anything but cash.[2] If such vendors will not accept a traveler's check, there is little chance they will accept your personal check or agree to bill you later. Many people find it prudent to always keep a $20, $50, or even a $100 bill tucked in with their driver's license to be used only for emergencies. To them, the cost from possible theft, loss, or accident and from interest foregone is far outweighed by the convenience of having this handy cash reserve at their fingertips.

A third benefit lies in the many discounts offered to those who pay with cash. Some restaurants and motels and an increasing number of professionals—plumbers, electricians, and doctors—give substantial discounts because of the high cost of billing and the problems of delinquent accounts and bad checks. For those who buy with cash, a 5 percent restaurant discount on even one meal could compensate for the liquidity cost of holding $50 in cash for the whole year. In addition, professional services frequently offer discounts as high as 20 percent, a very substantial benefit of using cash.

Finally, perhaps the most important benefit of carrying and using cash is related to its anonymity as a medium of exchange. Quite simply, there need be no record or proof of purchase when you use cash. This may be desirable for such innocent purchases as a birthday present whose price you want to keep secret. Part of the fun of giving your spouse a present may be lost if he or she sees what you paid when the checks or charge slips come back at the end of the month.

However, the anonymity benefit of using cash is also related to purchases that might later come back to haunt you. A canceled check or credit card slip showing $25 paid to Fantasy Car Wash, "Chicago's only adult car wash," might cause you considerable embarrassment when your spouse finds it among some other papers. Similarly, hard proof of some other purchases might cause you to lose your job or a possible job opportunity. If there are some purchases you do not want on the records, then you had better pay with cash.

Cash is also desired for the anonymity it provides as a way of storing personal wealth. Nobody can know how much you have unless they know where you have hidden it. Cash leaves no paper trail; it is not recorded in bankbooks; it is not recorded with the government. It can be used as you see fit, without the approval or knowledge of anybody else, including family and friends. Stored cash is usually not found when personal wealth is confiscated by the government (in tax cases), by the courts (in liability litigation), by nursing homes (as a precondition for admittance), and by spouses (as in divorce cases). Textbooks dwell on the costs and dangers of hoarding cash and frown on the benefits as being miserly or otherwise socially undesirable. However, given the large amount of cash being stored by individuals in our society, these benefits are obviously important and should be recognized. In many instances, holding assets in the form of cash may be the optimal way to preserve personal wealth and the freedom that it provides.

While using cash has its definite advantages, most transactions are made with money in the form of a personal check.

CHECKING ACCOUNT BALANCES

Checking account balances are almost as liquid as cash. They are called *demand deposits* because they may be withdrawn from the bank at any time on demand. The demand is most often made by writing a check. The person receiving the check can then "negotiate" it, i.e., cash it or deposit it and cause your account to be reduced by the amount specified. For most bills and purchases, checks are used instead of cash. Indeed, checking account balances and cash are such close substitutes that both are considered as part of the money supply.

The advantage of holding liquid balances in a checking account instead of in cash is that checks are safer and more convenient for large purchases. It is obviously easier to write and mail a check for $89.99 for a gas and electric bill than it is to mail the same amount in cash or coins or pay the bill in person. It is also safer; if a check is lost or stolen, the bank can be notified and payment stopped so that your account will not be affected.

Checking account balances are also safe from bank failure. Only a few small banks are not insured by the Federal Deposit Insurance Corporation, better known as

FDIC. Each account is insured up to $100,000. (If you have more than this amount, you might consider opening a second account in another bank also insured by FDIC.)

Another attraction of paying by check is that you have a permanent record that payment was actually made. This is a very important reason for using a checking account, particularly considering the frequency of mistakes associated with computerized billing, mistakes that can often be easily rectified if you can establish proof of payment. It is also important for proving deductions taken in computing income taxes.

One disadvantage of a checking account may be its transactions costs. Many banks charge a fee, typically 10 to 15 cents, for each check you write. Some banks charge for the checks themselves (particularly if a scenic picture or your photograph is printed on them). In addition, there are other service charges—for inactive accounts, balances below a specified minimum, and stop-payment orders—all of which can easily cost $50 or more per year for a typical individual or family.

A second disadvantage may be, ironically, the illiquidity cost of using checks as compared to using cash or credit cards. Checks on out-of-town banks may not be cashable and are often not even acceptable for payment of purchases.

A third disadvantage of a checking account is its liquidity cost. Like holding cash, keeping balances in a checking account means that you (usually) earn no interest. The interest foregone is the opportunity cost of being liquid. This opportunity cost is largely reduced if you switch from a regular checking account to a NOW account. (For an excellent, readable summary on checking accounts and how to rate them, see "Getting a Fair Deal on Your Checking," *Consumer Reports,* July 1988, pp. 455–463.)

NOW ACCOUNTS

NOW stands for "negotiable order of withdrawal"; it is like a check, except that it is an "order to withdraw" money from an interest-bearing account instead of a "demand to withdraw" it from a non-interest-bearing account. From 1972 to 1980, NOW accounts were available only from savings banks in New England and a few other states. After the Monetary Control Act of 1980, these interest-earning checking accounts have been available nationwide.

There is no physical difference between a check and a negotiable order of withdrawal; they look the same and can be used to pay bills and make purchases in the same way. The only real difference is that most NOW accounts pay 5 to 5.5 percent interest, which reduces the liquidity cost of holding cash or checking account balances. However, NOW accounts also have drawbacks. Most require that a substantial minimum balance be kept in the account, and some also impose high service charges if more than a small number of checks are drawn.

In 1983, super-NOW accounts were introduced. These promise to pay "market rate" interest, which is usually higher than 5.5 percent. A super-NOW account allows unlimited check writing but requires a higher minimum balance than does a regular NOW account.

STOP-PAYMENTS, OVERDRAFTS, AND BANKING BY MAIL

The use of checking accounts and NOW accounts can provide you with services that are not provided to those who prefer to use cash. One of these is the ability to stop payment even after you have handed over or mailed someone your check. From the time you write the check until the time it is cleared at your bank (i.e., deducted from your checking account balance), the check is "negotiable" but not yet "negotiated." During this period of time, you can request, usually for a fee of $10 to $15, that your bank render the check nonnegotiable; i.e., you instruct your bank not to honor the check. Such a stop-payment option gives you time to reconsider the transaction or to back out of it, as in the case of defective merchandise.

Suppose you have the "opportunity" to have your driveway sealed by an unknown company that has just completed several other jobs in the area. The cost is $150, but you must decide immediately, because "there is just enough sealer to do your driveway and the company is about to leave the area to do new jobs and won't be able to get back to your area this season." You agree and sign a contract. The job is completed and you pay with a check, even though a substantial discount is offered for payment in cash. That evening you hear a local television reporter warn consumers against falling for the driveway sealer scam. You examine your driveway and find that instead of the high-quality sealer you thought you were getting, your driveway was fraudulently brushed with kerosene and used motor oil. Finding and successfully suing the bogus company is highly unlikely. At least you can call your bank, however, and for a $10 fee, you can stop payment on your $150 check.

Another service available to most checking and NOW account holders is the ability to write checks (or drafts) for more than their current balance. This overdraft feature usually means that instead of "bouncing" a check written on insufficient funds and making a service charge, the bank automatically lends you multiples of, say, $100 that are added to your balance. The overdraft privilege is only available up to a certain amount, such as $500 or $1000.

An overdraft option is valuable for people who are careless in keeping track of their checking account balances. It saves embarrassment, inconvenience, and additional charges often levied by the person or business to whom you gave the bad check in the first place. The option is also valuable as a source of ready credit for emergencies or unforseen opportunities such as a special closeout sale. To this extent, it serves as a substitute for cash balances held for precautionary reasons. It is a cost-free (until used) line of credit.

The principal disadvantage of the overdraft option is the interest cost on overdraft borrowing. Nevertheless, the interest cost is competitive with other kinds of short-term loans, such as credit-card cash advances, and it is far less than money borrowed from finance companies, such as Beneficial or Household Finance. The only other disadvantage is the temptation to overspend and unnecessarily extend personal debt just because you have the ability to "write yourself an instant loan."

The third feature of checking and NOW accounts is the ability to bank by mail. This saves time and inconvenience and thereby lowers the cost of making transactions. (Of course, it would be possible to send cash by mail, but this is too risky and provides no sure record of the transaction.) It also provides you with use of the money, and hence the opportunity to earn interest, between the time you write a check and the time it is cleared. This is called *float*. Moreover, banking by mail allows you to get better service than local banks often provide. As a result, it promotes competition and better service for all consumers. For example, New York consumers were getting interest on their New England NOW accounts for 5 years before they were offered this service by their own banks. Banking out of town may not be "patriotic," but it can be profitable.

Even if you use an out-of-town bank because you get better service and/or earn higher interest rates, it is still wise to maintain a local checking account. Often local merchants are reluctant to cash out-of-town checks. Maintaining a local account—especially one with an overdraft option—solves this problem, since you can usually put out-of-town checks through your local account or simply cash them at the bank. You might also "connect" the two accounts with electronic banking.

Automated teller machines (ATMs) allow you to withdraw cash from your account almost anywhere day or night. They are convenient and easy to use. ATMs allow you to do many kinds of banking without waiting in line at the bank. Many people, particularly college students, use them several times each week.

In spite of their convenience, some people, particularly older people, avoid using ATMs. They are reluctant to try them, perhaps because they are less familiar with keyboarding and interacting with a computer or perhaps because they prefer to deal with human tellers. Such persons also may fear robbery or resent punching in access codes where the possibility exists that others who are standing nearby may steal them.

CERTIFIED, CASHIER'S, AND TRAVELER'S CHECKS

It is one thing to accept a check in payment for goods or services; it is another to be sure that the check can be negotiated—in other words, to be sure that the check is good or will not "bounce." If you buy a car or another big-ticket item from someone who does not know you, that person or company is likely to require payment in cash, with a certified check, or with a cashier's check.

To *certify a check,* you simply write out a regular check and take it to your bank. The bank immediately debits your account and stamps the check to indicate that sufficient funds have been set aside to ensure that the check will not "bounce." For a small service charge, the bank has guaranteed that funds are available to cover the check.

A *cashier's check* is one written on the bank's own account. Again, for a small service charge, the bank writes a check to whomever you wish for whatever amount you paid. It is a popular misconception that certified and cashier's checks are not subject to stop-payment orders. This is not true. If they are lost, stolen, or otherwise subject to an "adverse claim," you may request that the bank stop payment on them. However, stop-payments are not possible in cases where you receive defective merchandise unless a court restraining order is issued (which is usually impossible to execute before the check is cleared).

Traveler's checks are also guaranteed and, hence, are more easily accepted than are personal checks. The party accepting a traveler's check is never concerned about sufficient funds to cover the check. Nor is the acceptor subject to a discount on the check, as is the case for credit-card purchases. Traveler's checks can be purchased from American Express, Barclays, Thomas Cook, Bank of America, and a few other large banks.

A fee is often charged to the purchaser of traveler's checks. (American Express charges 1 percent, or $10 per $1000 worth of checks; Barclays and other traveler's checks have no initial purchase fee.) The checks are guaranteed against theft or loss and are not valid until countersigned. Because they are readily accepted and safe, traveler's checks are ideal for those who are frequently out of the area in which they live and bank.

With low service charges when they are purchased and with no service charges when they are cashed (except for small "processing fees" sometimes charged abroad), how can traveler's checks be profitable for the companies and banks that issue them? The answer lies in the time during which the issuing company or bank has your money at zero interest cost. They invest this money from the time you buy the traveler's checks until the time when the merchants to whom you give the checks cash them in. No wonder American Express urges you to always keep a few traveler's checks on hand even when you are not traveling. "Don't leave home without them, and if you have any when you return, don't hurry to cash them in." For the holder of traveler's checks, they provide liquidity and security at the price of interest foregone had the money been left in a NOW account, a savings account, or an investment. (In May of 1980, the American Bankers Club in Virginia began to market interest-bearing traveler's checks known as "ABC Security Plus Interest.")

We turn now to another kind of checking account not offered by either banks or nonbanks; it is checking on balances held with money market mutual funds. Later we shall return to banks and other savings institutions and examine their passbook accounts, certificates of deposit, and other liquid-asset offerings.

MONEY MARKET MUTUAL FUNDS

A *money market mutual fund* is a company whose principal assets consist of highly liquid, large-denomination, short-term debts, such as the securities issued by (or guaranteed by) the federal government or its agencies, certificates of deposit and bankers' acceptances issued by large banks, and some commercial paper issued by "gilt-edged stable corporations whose debts are rated no. 1 by established rating services, like Moody's and Standard & Poor's."[3] The liabilities of a money market mutual fund are the shares owned by investors whose money was used to buy these assets. Of course, the fund is also liable for its management fees and operation costs. In short, a money market mutual fund is a corporation that pools the money of small investors and uses it to buy low-risk, highly liquid securities.

One of the advantages of owning shares in a money market mutual fund is that the interest paid to a shareholder is just slightly less than that paid on the highest-grade, large-denomination borrowings. (The interest is slightly less because the fund takes a management fee, usually ½ to 1 percent of its total assets.) Without buying shares in a money market mutual fund, it is virtually impossible for most investors to add high-interest $1 million CDs, $5 million IBM notes, or large bankers' acceptances to their portfolios.

Although most money market funds require a minimum initial investment ranging from $1000 to $10,000, there are usually no charges to invest, reinvest, or redeem (cash in) one's shares. In other words, there are no direct commissions, so you can use the fund like a deposit-by-mail savings account.

A third advantage is available to shareholders whose money market mutual funds allow them to redeem their shares by writing checks. This permits you to write checks on your balance in the fund and still earn interest until the moment the check is cleared at the fund. To avoid the problem of processing millions of small checks, the money market mutual funds usually require that redemption checks be written for $250 or more.

With a check-writing option, a money market mutual fund becomes a checking account that pays interest. As such, it is comparable to a NOW account, except that (1) the checks must be written for more than a minimum amount and (2) the funds are not insured by the government for up to $100,000, as are most bank deposits. (This lack of insurance is not usually a concern to investors, since the securities in most money market funds are either backed by the government or by a major bank or corporation. Moreover, they are short-term debts their issuers will have to pay soon, before most of their other debts are due.) There is some risk, however, from mismanagement or embezzlement by the funds' managers, but this risk is considered by most experts to be very small.

Like a NOW account draft, a check drawn on a money market mutual fund allows balances to earn interest until the check is actually presented at the fund. You can continue to earn interest while the check is floating, i.e., from the time you write the check until the time it is cleared at the fund and deducted from your account.

A fourth advantage offered by some funds is the opportunity to make withdrawals by phone. Using a "password" or some other identification, you can instruct the fund to immediately transfer, say, $10,000 to your checking account or to some other predetermined, approved account. A toll-free number is usually provided by the fund, so the marginal cost of the transfer to the depositor is very low or nothing.

Finally, some money market mutual funds allow their shareholders to transfer part or all of their shares to other mutual funds promising higher rates of return. Again, there is usually no charge for this service. When the stock market is falling, you might like to stay in a safe money market fund (the speculative motive) and be satisfied with the 6 to 10 percent it is paying. But if you think the market will rise, you might like to switch to a fund whose assets are more risky but promise higher returns as well. The ease of switching between funds with a simple letter (or with a telephone call) and no transaction costs is another advantage offered by some money market mutual funds.

Although unheard of before 1972, money market mutual funds have become a widely accepted vehicle for managing cash reserves in the short run. They are a means of keeping assets very liquid and still earning some day-to-day interest. Let's now turn back to banks and savings institutions and see the interest they offer on other deposits that are liquid—although not as liquid as checking accounts, NOW accounts, and money market mutual fund accounts.

SAVINGS ACCOUNTS

A passbook savings account is the most commonly held asset in most individuals' and families' financial planning. A *savings account* is a time deposit, a deposit that will presumably be left in the bank for a period of time during which it will earn interest. Savings accounts can be opened at commercial banks or at other depository institutions such as savings banks, savings and loan associations, and credit unions. The rates vary, so if you keep substantial amounts in savings accounts, it pays to shop for the best rate.

By law, savings accounts can require a 30- to 90-day notice before they have to release your deposits. This requirement is virtually never imposed, unless you have made recent deposits with checks that have not yet cleared. To the extent that it does exist, however, it makes savings deposits more illiquid than checking deposits, which banks must pay on demand.

A second cost traditionally associated with savings deposits is the requirement to present your passbook each time a withdrawal is made. The inconvenience and cost of each transaction have generally been higher than the transaction costs associated with a checking account. But technology and innovation in the banking industry have lowered transaction costs for many savers. Direct deposit of paychecks (or portions of paychecks) has eliminated many Friday afternoon trips to the bank and waiting in line. Telephone transfers to and from checking accounts also have reduced the need to run to the bank. Finally, on-line computer accounting procedures are sending the old passbooks to the monetary museum. They are being replaced with plastic access cards for remote banking terminals (ATMs) and with simple monthly printouts showing all deposits, withdrawals, interest, and service charges.

Many of these savings innovations came after consumers began to substitute NOW accounts for regular savings accounts. NOW accounts pay only slightly lower rates than do savings accounts, and for many people, the convenience of being able to write checks makes NOW accounts more attractive overall.

Savings deposits are a popular place to hold cash being saved for a particular planned expenditure. Small deposits can be made, and when their sum is enough, the funds can be withdrawn easily. Such cash accumulation and holding is based on the finance motive, i.e., saving to spend for a particular good or service.

Savings deposits are also an attractive place to hold cash for the precautionary motive. Here liquid balances are held for an emergency or in the event that a good deal can be taken advantage of only if cash is available on short notice. To prevent the need to cash in other assets in a hurry or at an unfavorable time, savings balances provide protection against being illiquid.

For those who will not need their savings for a longer period and who do not mind holding less liquid assets, most banks and nonbanks offer other time deposits, such as certificates of deposit (CDs) and money market deposit accounts (MMDAs). Before we look at these, however, let's first see how interest on any kind of time deposit might be calculated.

Interest Calculation

In the simplest case, the dollar amount of interest earned on a time-deposit account is equal to the interest rate multiplied by the principal balance in the account. That is,

$$\text{Interest earned} = \text{interest rate} \times \text{account balance}$$

Conceptual and computational problems arise in deciding on how often interest will be computed (and added on to the previous balance) and in deciding what part of the balance will be "eligible" to earn interest. Professor Richard L. D. Morse of Kansas State University reports over 100 different ways of figuring interest earnings on a simple savings account.

Compounding Interest

Compounding means that previous interest earnings are included in the balance eligible to earn more interest. Thus the earnings for the period are figured on a balance that includes earnings from previous periods. Interest may be compounded annually, semiannually, quarterly, weekly, daily, or continuously. The more frequently interest is compounded, the higher the annual percentage yield can become; this is expressed as a percentage of the amount by which your original deposit will grow in

1 year. A nominal rate of 5 percent can yield up to 5.1271 percent depending on the method of compounding: annually—5.000 percent; semiannually—5.0625 percent; quarterly—5.0945 percent; weekly—5.1241 percent; daily—5.1267 percent; and continuously—5.1271 percent.

The formula for compounding is

$$\left(1 + \frac{r}{\text{number of periods per year}}\right)^{\text{number of periods per year}}$$

Therefore, for 5 percent compounded quarterly, we would have

$$\left(1 + \frac{0.05}{4}\right)^4$$

which is 1.050945. Therefore,

$$r = 5.0945 \text{ percent}$$

There is a considerable difference between interest compounded annually and interest compounded daily, but the difference between daily and continuous compounding is minuscule. For example, at 5 percent, the difference is less than half a cent on a $1000 deposit left in for the whole year. Banks that advertise continuous compounding as if it were something special compared to daily compounding are giving more hype than information.

Computing Interest Earnings

One of the most favorable methods of computing interest earnings is the *day-of-deposit to day-of-withdrawal method*. (This is also known as the *day-in to day-out, or DIDO, method.*) It is not only preferable that deposits be counted from the time they are made until the time they are withdrawn, but it is also preferable (1) that interest on them is compounded daily *and* (2) that it is paid daily. This latter distinction is tricky. Some interest is computed daily (and called *daily interest*), but it is only added to your balance at the end of the quarter. If money is drawn out before the end of the quarter, that money's interest is not paid to your account.

For example, let's look at an account whose balance is $1000 on January 1. The account has a nominal interest rate of 5 percent; its interest is compounded daily; its interest is paid daily; and its balance is computed by the DIDO method. The account had deposits and withdrawals for the quarter as shown in Table 2.1.[4] The exact steps used to calculate the balances for this account are shown in Table 2.2. Under our four assumptions, the interest earned for the quarter from January 1 to April 1 is $38.03.

Variations in DIDO Computations

There are at least three reasons why a 5 percent DIDO savings account with these same deposits and withdrawals might leave you with a higher balance than $2038.03, i.e., with more interest earned than $38.03:

1. *Grace days*. Some institutions allow you to earn interest from the first of the month for deposits made until the tenth of the month. The deposit on January 10

Table 2.1 Changes in a Savings Account During One Quarter

	Deposit	Withdrawal	Balance
Jan. 1	Beginning of quarter		$1000.00
Jan. 10	$2000		3001.23
Feb. 6	1000		4012.35
Mar. 5		$1000	3027.77
Mar. 20		500	2534.00
Mar. 30		500	2037.47
Apr. 1	Beginning of next quarter		$2038.03

Table 2.2 Computation of the Interest Earned and New Balance for Changes Shown in Table 2.1

Date	Days to Next Balance	Interest Earned per $100	Activity	Balance
Jan. 1:			Balance	$1,000.00
	9 days	12.34¢	Earns	+ 1.23
Jan. 10:			Deposit	+ 2,000.00
				= $3,001.23
	27 days	37.05¢	Earns	+ 11.12
Feb. 6:			Deposit	+ 1,000.00
				= $4,012.35
	28 days*	38.43¢	Earns	+ 15.42
Mar. 5:			Withdrawal	− 1,000.00
				= $3,027.77
	15 days	20.57¢	Earns	+ 6.23
Mar. 20:			Withdrawal	− 500.00
				= $2,534.00
	10 days	13.71¢	Earns	+ 3.47
Mar. 30:			Withdrawal	− 500.00
				= $2,037.47
	2 days	2.74¢	Earns	+ .56
Apr. 1:			Balance	= $2,038.03

Source: *Richard L. D. Morse*, Check Your Interest (*Manhattan, Kansas: Morse Publications, 1978*), p. 3.
*Leap year.

would have earned $2.50 more and the one on February 6 would have earned $0.69 more, bringing the total interest to $41.22.

2. *Dead days*. Some institutions ignore deposits and withdrawals made during a couple of days at the end of the quarter when they are computing the earnings. Thus the $500 withdrawal on March 30 may have been ignored.

3. *Use of 360-day basis*. A higher daily rate is paid for the same nominal 5 percent quoted annual percentage rate (APR) because each day's rate is $\frac{1}{360}$ (not $\frac{1}{365}$) of 5.00 percent. About 74 cents more would be earned each year with the 360-day basis per $1000 in the account.

While the interest earned could be higher than the $38.03 shown in Table 2.2, it is much more likely to be lower. Here are some of the common pitfalls that reduce interest below the DIDO compounded-daily example shown in the table:

1. *Service charges*. Some accounts are charged penalties, such as for an account where more than a maximum number of deposits and/or withdrawals are made within the quarter.

2. *LIFO method*. This assumes that the money last deposited is the first money to be withdrawn (last-in, first-out; LIFO) and that these withdrawals cancel the interest earned on the earlier deposits. In our example,

the LIFO method would reduce the interest earned to $23.84.

3. *FIFO method.* This assumes that the money first deposited is canceled by withdrawals (first-in, first-out; FIFO). (If the first deposit is not enough, the remainder is taken from subsequent deposits.) This would reduce interest in our example to $20.10.

4. *Use of 360-day basis.* A higher daily rate is paid for the same nominal 5 percent annual percentage rate (APR) because each day's rate is ⅟₃₆₀, instead of ⅟₃₆₅, of 5.00 percent:

$$\left(1 + \frac{0.05}{360}\right)^{365} \quad \text{compared to} \quad \left(1 + \frac{0.05}{365}\right)^{365}$$

5. *Low balance.* The most damaging method of computation of all is if the interest is computed only on the lowest balance. In our example, this low balance would be $1000; for the 91 days in the quarter, the interest earned would be only $12.54. About 80 percent of banks employ this method of interest computation for their interest-bearing checking accounts, such as NOW accounts and MMDA accounts.

6. *Rounding balances.* Balances rounded off to the next lowest dollar mean less interest for the depositor. Credit unions often round off to the next lowest $5 share.

Most people are unaware of the large variations in interest earned on time-deposit accounts. They often feel that "the difference of a quarter of a percent in interest is not worth hassling about." As we have seen, however, the differences can be far greater as a result of the computation methods employed than any small interest-rate variations might imply.

CERTIFICATES OF DEPOSIT

A *certificate of deposit* (*COD* or *CD*) is a receipt certifying that a certain amount of money has been deposited at the bank issuing the certificate. The certificate also specifies the rate of interest and the date on which the principal deposit and interest may be withdrawn, i.e., the date on which the CD matures. In other words, a CD is really a loan made by you to the bank for which you receive interest.

In the early 1960s, a few aggressive banks in New York City sought to attract more depositors by offering certificates that paid higher rates of interest than could be earned on regular passbook savings accounts. In return for these higher rates, the depositor was required (1) to make a large deposit and (2) not to withdraw it for a certain number of years. The larger the deposit—meaning the larger the CD—and the longer the time until maturity, the higher was the interest rate offered by the bank.

Prior to 1986, the government set maximum interest rates that banks were allowed to pay on CDs. These *interest-rate ceilings* or *usury rates* were supposed to prevent banks from becoming overly competitive in their attempts to attract depositors' funds. In restricting the interest paid on deposits, however, these maximum rates

inhibited straightforward competition in the banking industry to the detriment of depositors, particularly small
depositors. There was no ceiling imposed on very rich
depositors who bought certificates of $100,000 or more.
The ceilings also hindered banks from competing with
money-market mutual funds, whose rates were never
regulated.

It is also interesting to note that the CDs issued by
many banks no longer look like certificates at all; they
look like regular savings account passbooks. When a
withdrawal is made, these passbooks must be presented
at the bank or savings institution. Depositors who wish
to make early withdrawals, i.e., withdrawals prior to
maturity of the CDs, suffer interest penalties. On CDs of
12 months and less, savers who withdraw the principal
early lose 3 months' worth of interest; on CDs with
longer maturities, they would lose 6 months' worth of
interest. (The interest may be withdrawn monthly as it
is earned with no penalty.) It is not wise to buy a CD
unless you expect to be able to hold it until maturity.

MONEY MARKET DEPOSIT ACCOUNTS

In late 1981, banks and other depository institutions began to offer money market deposit accounts (MMDAs)
in an effort to compete with the increasingly popular
money market mutual funds. These types of savings deposits offered current money market rates of interest (no
interest ceilings were imposed), initial deposits of less
than $5000 (most were only $500), and the opportunity
to make up to six withdrawals each month (three by

check and three by automatic transfer, e.g., to pay a mortgage).

MMDAs have taken back some deposits that were lost to the money market mutual funds. For one thing, people like them because they are offered where they already have checking and savings accounts. A second reason is that MMDAs are federally insured (at banks by FDIC and at savings and loans by FSLIC). However, MMDAs generally pay less than money market mutual funds, and withdrawals are still limited to six per month.

More will be said about MMDAs and other savings deposits and certificates issued by banks and other depository institutions, but first let's take a look at liquid securities offered directly by the U.S. government. The most popular of these securities is U.S. Savings Bonds.

U.S. SAVINGS BONDS

U.S. Savings Bonds are relatively small denomination securities issued by the federal government to provide the common person with a safe, convenient place to save. Approximately one out of every three American households owns Savings Bonds, and more than 16 million people buy them yearly. They also provide the government with a medium of spreading the public debt to people in lower income and wealth classes—people who would not ordinarily buy stocks, bonds, and other securities.

Savings Bonds currently come in two types: Series EE and Series HH. Series EE bonds are issued in denominations of $50, $75, $100, $200, $500, $1000, $5000, and $10,000. They are issued at 50 percent of face value and mature in 10 years. Interest accrues on these bonds, but it is not receivable or taxable until the bonds are redeemed or cashed in. No interest is earned, nor can the Series EE bonds be redeemed during the first 6 months after they are purchased. After that, the interest grows at 85 percent of the average rate on 5-year Treasury securities as long as the bonds are not cashed in before 5 years. In other words, every 6 months the Savings Bond rates are set at 85 percent of the average rate on 5-year Treasury securities. After a bond is 5 years old, the ten semiannual averages are added, averaged, and compounded to determine the bond's value. In no case, however, is the compound annual rate (after 5 years) less than the guaranteed minimum rate when the bond was purchased. For example, the guaranteed minimum rate was 7½ percent for those purchased in April of 1986; in 1989, the guaranteed minimum rate had fallen to 6 percent, even though the Savings Bonds were expected to yield 7.35 percent.

Series HH bonds are available in larger denominations: $500, $1000, $5000, and $10,000 only through the exchange of Series EE bonds. Unlike the Series EE bonds, the interest is sent to the bondholder every 6 months. This feature makes them attractive to some retired people who want to use their wealth holdings to produce a steady source of income. Also, the income tax on interest accrued on the Series EE bonds that were exchanged for the Series HH bonds is deferred until the Series HH bonds are finally cashed in.

There are several advantages to purchasing and holding U.S. Savings Bonds.

1. *Small denominations.* Most corporate bonds sell in multiples of $1000.

2. *Easy availability.* Savings Bonds can be purchased at most commercial banks or other savings institutions or through banks from the Federal Reserve or the Bureau of Public Debt.

3. *No transactions cost.* There is no charge made when buying or selling Series EE bonds. (A small redemption charge is levied for Series HH bonds, however.)

4. *Virtually no risk of default.* Both the interest and the principal are guaranteed by the federal government.

5. *Low risk of loss.* The bonds are registered and can be replaced if lost or destroyed by fire, theft, or whatever.

6. *Tax deferral.* Federal taxes on interest earned on Series EE bonds is deferred until the bonds are redeemed. (Redemption also can be delayed past the maturity date and if they are exchanged for Series HH bonds.) The deferral feature can make Savings Bonds particularly attractive to people approaching retirement. You can save now, when you are in a high tax bracket, and hold off paying income taxes until after retirement, when your tax bracket may be lower.

7. *Tax exemption.* Interest earned on savings bonds is exempt from state, local, or personal property taxes.

8. *"Forced" saving.* Payroll-deduction plans are

often set up so money can be used to buy U.S. Savings Bonds in the worker's name. (There is no rule to prevent these deductions from going into each worker's savings account, but if this were the case, workers would be more apt to withdraw and spend it.)

However, there are also some serious disadvantages that may make Savings Bonds unattractive to careful investors—even to those with very small investment portfolios:

1. *Low interest.* Only 6.0 percent is currently guaranteed on U.S. Savings Bonds. Even less is paid if the bonds are not held at least 5 years.

2. *Nonnegotiable (nonmarketable).* Savings Bonds may not be transferred or sold to another person, as most conventional bonds can. Nor can they be used as collateral for a loan.

3. *Initial illiquidity.* Series EE Savings Bonds may not be redeemed at all for the first 6 months after they are purchased.

4. *Maximum purchase.* No more than $30,000 worth of Savings Bonds may be purchased in any 1 year. (This is not a serious problem, since most people with this amount of money could find other equally desirable savings assets.)

The biggest advantages of holding Savings Bonds are their (partial) tax-exempt status and their ability (at least for Series EE) to allow taxes on the interest accumulated to be deferred until the bonds are redeemed. However, these features are most attractive to upper-income people—the very people who are likely to find Savings Bonds to be less desirable when compared with (1) the higher-interest returns, (2) the liquidity, and (3) the collateral value of most time deposits offered by commercial banks and savings institutions.

Still, for those who are concerned with their investments' safety and for those who believe that buying Savings Bonds is "buying stock in America," they do provide a reasonable form of investment. (The Freedom Shares, special Series E bonds sold during the Vietnam war, were largely purchased by people who believed that buying them supported the war and the boys overseas. The lower rate of return was somewhat compensated for by the patriotic act of purchasing them.) Savings Bonds are also a "good investment" for those who need the discipline of a payroll-deduction method of saving, although, again, there may be better investments that could be made in connection with such "forced" saving.

For investors with at least $10,000 who want a very safe, short-term security, there is the opportunity to purchase other, more negotiable forms of government debt.

U.S. TREASURY DEBT

When the United States government borrows money, its IOUs are called *bills, notes,* or *bonds.* Treasury IOUs issued with maturities of 1 year or less (i.e., due within

1 year) are called *Treasury bills*. IOUs for more than 1 year and up to 10 years are called *Treasury notes*. When the Treasury borrows for 10 years or more, its debts are simply referred to as *government bonds*.

Treasury bills (T-bills) are issued with maturities of 3, 6, and 12 months and are sold in minimum amounts of $10,000 and multiples of $5000 above that minimum. Unlike Savings Bonds aimed at individual savers, T-bills were intended to be sold to banks, corporations, and other institutions, such as pension funds. However, individuals can purchase newly issued T-bills directly at thirty-seven Federal Reserve Banks and branches around the country or indirectly through most banks and brokerage houses. Direct purchase is time-consuming and complicated, but there is no fee. Banks and brokers generally charge $25 to $50 for a $10,000 T-bill.

All three kinds of government debt provide their investors with the highest degree of security against default. It is (almost) inconceivable that our federal government would ever welsh on its debts when they become due. Even if taxes and other revenues were insufficient to pay these debts, the government could always issue new debts to cover the ones now due. The government also could print money, which is equivalent to non-interest-bearing government debt. (A $100 bill is equivalent to a $100 government IOU that bears no interest.)

Treasury debt is also negotiable. There is an active secondary market for Treasury bills, notes, and bonds.

These securities differ with respect to interest rate, face value, and maturity date. The price of each type of security depends on the forces of supply and demand—just as in any other free market.

Treasury bills used to be offered as tangible certificates that looked like any other security. In the early 1970s, there was a switch to *book-entry bills,* meaning that depositors now receive only a receipt for their purchases of Treasury debt, not a nicely printed, formal certificate. This book-entry system saves time and printing costs and frees the Treasury and buyers from handling and possibly losing tangible securities. Some investors do not feel right, however, unless they physically possess the government's written IOU.

The interest earned on a Treasury bill is the difference between what you pay for it, say, $9500, and its maturity value, say, $10,000. What you pay for newly issued bills depends on auctions held every Monday (for 3- and 6-month bills) and every fourth Wednesday (for 12-month bills). So the rates are constantly changing. Like Savings Bonds, interest earned on Treasury debt is not subject to state and local income taxes or to personal property taxes. This can mean a tax saving of about 10 percent of the interest earned for residents of high local tax areas, such as New York City. Many people are under the mistaken belief that interest earned on Treasury debt is also free from federal income taxes. This is not true, however; the interest earned on Treasury bills, notes, and bonds is subject to federal taxation, and fail-

Table 2.3   A Comparison of a $10,000 U.S. Treasury Bill and a $10,000 Certificate of Deposit, Both Maturing in 6 Months

U.S. Treasury Bill, $10,000 Denomination	$10,000 Certificate of Deposit
Backed in full by the U.S. government insurance for up to $100,000	Almost always backed by federal government
May be sold at any time at the current market price; all forms of Treasury debt are negotiable	Not negotiable or transferable, but may be redeemed early with a 3-month loss of interest
Book entry only, no certificate or tangible bill issued (since 1976)	Actual savings certificate issued
No service charge if purchased directly from a Federal Reserve Bank or its branches, but if purchased through a bank or broker, a single 3-month $10,000 bill can cost from $25 to $70 and more	No service charge of any kind
Interest is subject to federal income taxes only	Interest is subject to federal, state, and local income taxes
Purchases can be made only in certain fixed amounts, i.e., $10,000 to buy the first bill and then additional amounts in multiples of $5000	Deposits can be made in any amounts over $10,000; i.e., you can buy a certificate for $11,000 or $12,500 or any other amount over $10,000

ure to report it is likely to flag your tax return for an audit.

Since Treasury bills and large certificates of deposit from a bank or savings institution are close alternative investments, be sure to compare them (see Table 2.3).

CHOOSING AMONG FINANCIAL INSTITUTIONS

There are three principal criteria for choosing one or more financial institutions to help you manage your liquid assets. They are convenience, kind and quality of service, and cost of service. There are no arbitrary rules for deciding if a commercial bank, savings bank, savings and loan association, credit union, or money-market mutual fund is best for you. But there are some basic points to consider.

The first is where to have a checking account. Some banks offer truly "free" checking insofar as they have

¶ No service charge per check
¶ No monthly service charge
¶ No charge for printing checks
¶ No minimum account balance

Although such "free" checking was very rare until the late 1960s, it is now quite easy to find, especially if you are a member of a large union, an employee of a large company, or an affiliate of some other organization with economic clout. It is even more preferable if interest is paid on the daily balance, as it is with most NOW accounts.

It is wise to compare checking account services at other banks and to periodically ask yourself these questions:

¶ Does my bank have convenient hours? (Some banks open at 8 A.M.; others have evening and weekend hours.)

¶ Does my bank have ATMs close by, and what does the bank charge for ATM service?

¶ Do I have to wait long in the bank or at the drive-in windows? Is there a closer banking facility?

¶ Can I bank by mail; if so, does the bank pay the postage? Postage-paid envelopes for banking are a mixed benefit. On one hand, you save the postage; on the other, they are not delivered as quickly as are first-class stamped envelopes, because the post office must record the permit numbers before they are delivered.

¶ Are my checks numbered? Are the checks listed on my monthly statement in the order that I wrote them?

¶ Is my name printed on each check? Is there a charge to print my address on each check?

¶ Can I make a direct deposit of my paycheck at this bank and thereby save rushing to the bank on payday?

¶ Can I deposit out-of-town checks and draw on them without being required to wait until they clear?

¶ Can I pay certain bills (such as mortgage and utility bills) by phone without having to write checks?

¶ Does my bank account make me eligible for a VISA or MasterCard credit card?

¶ Do I have an overdraft privilege; if so, how much is
it for and at what interest rate?

When managing larger cash balances that you want
to be able to spend with the stroke of a pen, a money
market mutual fund is probably preferable even to a local
NOW account. The rates of return among over 300
money market mutual funds vary daily, and no one fund
consistently outperforms the others. Therefore, service
and convenience are likely to be more important than is
any particular rate of return.

The second consideration is what service do you get
with your savings account. How much interest is paid,
and what type of accounts are offered? How is the interest computed? Is it compounded daily? How often is the
interest posted or paid to your account balance? In addition, you might also want to know if you can use your
savings account for collateral on a short-term loan? This
often allows people to borrow at lower rates than those
charged on regular personal loans.

Finally, you should consider the other services provided by financial institutions. Does your bank grant
home mortgages, car loans, or personal loans more readily to its regular customers? (This can be the most important reason for banking at a credit union.) Are safe
deposit boxes available, and what are the rates charged
on them? Are cashier's checks and traveler's checks
available to regular customers at preferred rates or with
no charge at all? Can you cash checks—both yours and
those made out to you but drawn on out-of-town banks?

A comparison of all these services will help you to select one bank or a combination of banks, nonbanks, and money market mutual funds that best suits your needs and desires in managing your liquid assets.

POINTS TO REMEMBER

¶ Cash is the most liquid asset you can hold. The benefits of holding cash include its usefulness in making small purchases, its service as a precautionary balance, its anonymity as a medium of exchange, and its discounts versus those offered (or not offered) for other means of payment. The disadvantages of holding cash include the risk of theft, loss, or accident and the opportunity cost of interest foregone.

¶ Checking accounts are primarily held as transactions balances. They are safe, convenient, and provide permanent records that payments were made. Their service charges and their lack of interest are the biggest drawbacks.

¶ NOW accounts are interest-bearing accounts; they can represent an improvement over checking deposits, providing their service charges do not exceed the interest they pay.

¶ Shares in money market mutual funds can serve as interest-bearing deposits. Most money market fund checks must be drawn for a minimum amount (e.g., at least $500), and they are not federally insured. Telephone-switching services may allow a shareholder to transfer money to another mutual fund or to transfer it to a commercial bank where the shareholder has a checking or savings account.

¶ The interest earned on savings accounts depends on the annual percentage rate, the method of compounding, and the length of time the money is left in the account.

¶ Certificates of deposit, U.S. Savings Bonds, and U.S. Treasury bills and notes provide savers with very low risk securities with various maturities. Savings Bonds and Treasury debts are not subject to state and local income taxes nor to personal property taxes.

¶ Choosing the correct financial institution to fit your needs is not only a question of which one costs the least or pays the most interest. Convenience and service are also very important.

3

STOCKS

The most common financial investments made by individuals are purchases of securities issued by corporations and governments usually for the purpose of expanding their output of goods and services. Since the money from the original sale of these securities is used mostly to buy real capital—that is, make investments in new buildings, machinery, assembly lines, roads, bridges, and basic research—the market for the securities themselves is known as the *capital market*. The capital market includes the markets for common stocks, for bonds maturing later than 1 year, and for preferred stocks. (A portion of the securities market, the one for securities maturing in 1 year or less, is known as the *money market*. As we saw in the last chapter, such short-term securities are issued by banks, other corporations, and governments, not to purchase capital, but to raise money for short-term needs.)

COMMON STOCKS, BONDS, AND PREFERRED STOCKS

A *common stock* is a certificate showing evidence of ownership in a corporation. Since *ownership* and *equity* are synonymous, stocks are often called *equities*.

A corporation is owned by its stockholders. If there

are 1 million shares of stock and you own 100 shares, then you own $\frac{1}{10,000}$ of the total corporation. As an owner, you have certain legal rights and privileges:

1. You have the *right to vote* in all corporate elections. For example, you have the right to vote for the board of directors who run the corporation.
2. You have a *right to your share of the dividends* paid by the corporation. *Dividends* are the portion of the corporation's earnings the board of directors has decided will be distributed. (The rest of the earnings go for taxes or are retained by the corporation for capital investment.)
3. You have a *right to your share of the residual value* of the corporation's assets in the event it goes bankrupt. The *residual* means that all debts and other corporate obligations must be paid first.
4. You have the *right to limited liability*; the most you can lose is the amount you spent to purchase the stock. This might seem unimportant, but owners of unincorporated businesses can be held liable beyond the value of the business. If you own stock in a utility corporation responsible for a nuclear disaster, the most you can lose is the value of the stock; you cannot be sued for anything beyond that.

Although a stock gives its holder a claim on the dollar value of the corporation, it does *not* grant any rights to the physical or financial assets of the corporation. A stockholder with 100 shares of a company with 1 million shares outstanding cannot decide to take $\frac{1}{10,000}$ of the corporate assets and sell them. The corporation has claims on its assets; stockholders merely have claims on the corporation.

Unlike an equity security (such as common stock), a *bond* is a certificate showing evidence of creditorship to a corporation (or debtorship by a corporation or government). A bond is simply a fancy IOU. It states the amount of the debt (the face value), the rate of interest, how often the interest will be paid, and the maturity date or when the debt itself (the principal) will be paid back. Most bonds have face values of $1000 or multiples of that amount.

Bondholders are creditors. They do not have equity or rights of ownership. However, they do have the right to payment of their debt before any dividends are paid, and in the event of bankruptcy, bondholders are paid before any stockholder.

A *preferred stock* is a cross between a stock and a bond. Like common stock, it is an equity, but like a bond, its holder receives a fixed periodic dividend specified in the certificate. As in the case of common stock, dividends can be withheld by the board of directors, but if this is done, no common stockholder of the same company can receive any dividends either. As a result, payment of the dividends on preferred stock is rather certain.

Like a bondholder, an owner of preferred stock usually does not have the right to vote in corporate elections. Nor do the returns on preferred stock increase when the company is expanding; as a result, there is little appreciation in the value of preferred stock. Finally, in the event of bankruptcy, preferred stockholders get their share after bondholders but before those who own common stock.

MAKING INVESTMENTS IN COMMON STOCKS

Common stocks are held by individuals for two main reasons: (1) the expectation of dividend income, and (2) the expectation of appreciation in the stocks' market value. In addition, some very wealthy people hold enough stock to be able to control the corporation; this may give them economic and political power that, in turn, can have value beyond the simple expectation of dividends and appreciation.

Dividends and capital gains (which are realized appreciation) still enjoy a tax advantage over earned income, insofar as neither is subject to Social Security taxes. Prior to 1987, the first $100 of dividends received each year ($200 for jointly owned stock) was completely tax free and only 40 percent of long-term capital gains was taxed; i.e., 60 percent was tax-free. The amount of capital gains that is taxable has been changed several times over the past two decades, and it is likely that some tax preference for capital gains will be reinstituted in the future. (President Bush has favored bringing back a portion of the capital gains exclusion, at least that portion representing capital lost due to inflation.)

Stocks of companies that are expected to grow rapidly may be referred to as *growth stocks*. Most of their earnings are retained and plowed back into the company. These stocks are attractive to people who hope to increase their wealth through rapid appreciation and who can forego any significant cash flow in the form of dividends. McDonalds, Polaroid, and Texas Instruments are prominent examples of corporations whose stocks can be called growth stocks (at least over the last decade).

Stocks that are traded in large volumes, that have good track records of providing steady dividends and steady appreciation, and that are expected to continue to do so are referred to as *blue-chip stocks*. They are shares in big, stable companies such as General Motors, International Business Machines, and Xerox.

There are also *cyclical stocks* (whose changes in market value tend to coincide with aggregate business fluctuations), *countercyclical stocks* (such as gold mine shares, whose values tend to rise as the rest of the market declines), *defensive stocks* (whose values are thought to hold constant against market declines), *mature-growth stocks, aggressive-growth stocks,* and other categories that are less well-defined but seem to fit a certain group for a certain period of time. While most investors agree that IBM is a blue-chip stock, there is little widespread agreement (and little profit) in fitting every stock into one of several rigid categories.

THE STANDARD & POOR'S 500 INDEX
The most popular of all gauges of overall performance in the stock market is the Standard & Poor's Composite

Index of 500 Stocks. This index is a weighted average of the following:

> 400 industrial stocks
>
> 40 utility stocks
>
> 40 financial stocks
>
> <u>20</u> transportation stocks
>
> 500 total

The average is weighted to reflect the opinions of a small number of Standard & Poor's Corporation employees who compose the 500 Committee. Stocks are occasionally added and deleted in accordance with the 500 Committee's perception of what best represents entire industries. (In 1976, for example, forty-six were added and forty-six others were deleted.)

Each of the 500 stocks is weighted according to the total current market value of its common stock relative to the average market value in some base period. Currently, the base period is 1941 to 1943. This base is given the index of 10.

The weight for the XYZ Company's stock is determined by dividing the total current market value of XYZ stock by the average total market value of XYZ stock from 1941 to 1943 and multiplying the result by 10. The current price of each company's stock times its weight is computed for all 500 companies, and the average of these weighted prices is the Standard & Poor's 500 Index. Electronic computers calculate this index at 5-minute intervals and report the closing index number at the end of each day.

THE OVER-THE-COUNTER MARKET

Of all the companies in this country, the stocks and bonds of approximately 3000 are traded often enough and in sufficient volume to be auctioned continuously on the registered stock and bond exchanges. The rest are traded by phone calls, by teletype, and by other electronic systems connecting thousands of securities brokers all over the country. There is no single physical marketplace. Instead, all the communication and (mostly electronic) transfer systems between securities dealers form the market known as the *over-the-counter market*.

The most frequently traded securities in this market are connected to a nationwide computer system, called the National Association of Securities Dealers' Automated Quotation System (NASDAQ), which was developed in the late 1960s. Dealers who are tied into this system can get continuous information on the prices at which some dealers are ready to sell and the prices at which others are willing to buy. The median price at which dealers are willing to buy is called the *bid price*; the median price at which others are willing to sell is called the *asked price*. All this information is computed continuously, and the end-of-the-day figures are published in the financial pages of most large newspapers.

For stocks, the name of the company, the dividend

(if any) per share, the total sales in 100s, the bid price, the asked price, and the change in the bid price from the previous trading day are all listed. If the paper shows

Stock & Div.	Sales 100s	Bid	Asked	Net Chg.
Acme Elec .24	8	7-1/4	8	. . .

this means that 800 shares of the Acme Electric Corporation, whose stock paid an annual dividend last year of 24 cents a share, were traded and that the median bid price was $7.25 and the median asked price was $8.00. The bid price of $7.25 was the same as it was at the close of the day before.

When you buy over-the-counter securities, your broker is likely to sell on a *net-price basis*. This means that you pay no commission, but you do pay more than the broker paid. The difference is the broker's *markup*. Similarly, when you sell on a net-price basis, the broker gives you less than he or she expects to get. The difference is called a *markdown*; it is the broker's profit, not a commission. As an individual—especially one making large trades—this difference means that you, acting as a buyer, should treat the broker as the seller and should negotiate the markup before you buy. (Acting as a seller, you should treat the broker as a buyer and negotiate the markdown before you sell.)

USING THE SERVICES OF A STOCKBROKER

Any corporation could sell you its stock directly. Any individual could sell you stock that he or she owns. But the information and other transactions costs involved in such direct buyer-seller exchanges make them impractical and the exception. In the securities market with thousands of different investments and millions of different buyers and sellers, efficiency is achieved through a few established marketplaces that handle the bulk of the securities exchanged.

Stockbrokers work for firms that own "seats" in these established marketplaces, such as the New York Stock Exchange. When you place an order with a stockbroker, he or she transmits that order to the floor of the particular exchange where that security is traded in an auction market. For example, IBM stock is traded on the New York Stock Exchange (NYSE) but not on the American Stock Exchange (AMEX). The trade is then executed, and often within minutes you receive confirmation of that transaction.

Organized securities exchanges make it easy for buyers and sellers to "find" each other and come to an agreement. By comparison, direct buyer-seller negotiation would be difficult, inconvenient, and inefficient. It is one thing to sell a used car on your own; a car is an indivisible, nonhomogeneous good with a value that falls in a subjective range from, say, $1000 to $1200 for a 10-year-old sedan with surface body rust. However, 100 shares of a particular stock constitute a divisible, homogeneous asset, each share of which is worth, for example, exactly $25.13 as of 10:15 A.M. last Friday. Again, the only practical way for an individual to sell (or buy) such an asset is through an organized exchange.

In addition to being indispensable middlemen, stockbrokers also provide more extensive services if you desire them. Briefly, they can

¶ Provide technical information on securities of interest to you
¶ Make recommendations of securities you "should" buy or sell
¶ Manage your portfolio of securities at their own discretion based on your prior written permission allowing them to do so
¶ Pay interest on cash balances left in your account held with them
¶ Lend you money to buy securities (known as buying securities *on margin*)

There is no guarantee that stockbrokers will make your portfolio grow. Historically, their performance as managers is rather suspect. Indeed, as we saw in Chapter 1, many people believe you could do better on your own with random selection.

There are, however, certain guarantees that brokers and the firms they represent will not go bankrupt and cause you to lose a portion or all of your account held with them. Investors are automatically insured up to $500,000 for securities and up to $100,000 for cash held with brokers who are members of the Securities Investors Protection Corporation (SIPC). Most large brokerage houses carry additional insurance as well.

PURCHASING STOCKS

There are different kinds of orders that you may place with a broker to take advantage of or protect against sudden changes in market prices. The simplest order—the one to buy or sell a stock—is called a *market order.* This is an order to buy (or sell) a certain number of shares at the best price after the order is presented on the floor of the exchange (New York, American, or wherever). For example, you tell your broker to buy 100 shares of IBM and expect to get it at the lowest price offered when your order reaches the floor of the New York Stock Exchange.

A more complicated order is the *limit order.* It is an order to buy (or sell) a certain number of shares at a specified or better price. For example, you tell your broker to buy fifty shares of AT&T if the price falls to $55 or below. This is used to capitalize on an expected temporary fall in price. Limit orders may be entered for a single trading day, a week, or a month, or they may be good until canceled (GTC). In the case of a limit order to sell, you tell your broker to sell 100 shares of Xerox if the price rises to $65 or above. This is used to capture an expected temporary gain in price.

A *stop order* to sell is designed to protect a gain or curb a loss. Here you tell the broker to sell RCA if the price falls to $21 or below. In this case, you have already made a gain, and you want to protect it from a sudden continued fall in price. There may be a complication, however. When a number of stop orders begin to cause sharp changes in price, the exchange might cancel all of them. At that point, you would have to resubmit the order as a regular market order to sell.

PAYING THE TRANSACTIONS COST OF STOCK INVESTMENTS

As a general rule, brokerage commissions from full-service brokers (such as Merrill Lynch, Bache Halsey Stuart Shields, Smith Barney, and Dean Witter) are about 2 percent of the value of the stocks purchased or sold depending on the number of shares and the price per share. Prior to 1975, these commission rates were fixed. Since then, competition, led by new "discount" brokers (such as Charles Schwab), has brought rates down, often below 1 percent.

Brokerage commissions are said to be negotiable. However, like a real estate broker's commission, the rates charged by a particular firm for small investors are fixed for all intents and purposes. Rates do vary among brokerage firms, however, and it pays to comparison-price shop, especially if you are an active trader. One company might not always be less expensive. Buying 200 shares of a stock at $20 per share might be cheaper at Merrill Lynch compared with the commission charged by Dean Witter, while at the same time buying 400 shares at $10 per share might be cheaper at Dean Witter compared with the commission charged by Merrill Lynch.

What these transactions costs mean to you, the investor, is that a stock must appreciate about 4 percent before it can be sold for a net profit (assuming there are about 2 percent fees to buy and 2 percent to sell and disregarding additional claims on money, such as dividends, which the stock may have paid while you held it). Transactions fees mean income to the broker and hence an incentive to urge you to buy or sell. When brokers push investors just to earn more commissions for themselves, they are said to be *churning* their clients' accounts.

For self-directed investors who know what they want and when to buy or sell, discount brokers (such as Charles Schwab, Quick & Reilly, Olde Discount Brokers, and Fidelity Brokerage Services) offer excellent service at about half the commission charged by a full-service broker for, say, a $5000 trade. Many discount brokers offer 24-hour service, monthly newsletters, free material from other investment advisory services (such as Value Line and Standard & Poor's), and toll-free phone calls for investors out of their area. Their representatives earn salaries, not commissions on how much they get you to buy or sell. They execute your orders, but they do not give you advice and try to persuade you to buy or sell so that they can earn commissions.

BUYING FOR CASH

Whenever you purchase a stock (or a bond), federal law requires that the purchase be paid by the *settlement date,* which is no more than 5 business days after the transaction. Failure to pay your broker before the settlement date means that the broker is required to sell the securities you ordered and hold you responsible for any loss to the brokerage firm plus commissions.

Similarly, whenever the stock is sold, the certificate must be delivered to your broker by the settlement date. Unless it is, you will not receive a check for the stock you sell, and moreover, your broker must buy back the securities. Again, you would be responsible for any loss that the brokerage firm incurs plus commissions.

It usually takes 4 to 6 weeks after the transaction to have stock certificates registered and delivered to you. Although you may not yet have the physical stock certificate, you are nevertheless entitled to sell the security, receive dividends, and vote from the moment after the transaction is settled.

Storing stock certificates and carrying them between your broker and your safe-deposit box can be inconvenient, especially if you are an active trader and have trouble taking time off from work to go to the bank and to the broker's office. It is more convenient for many investors to leave their securities registered in the brokerage firm's name, referred to as the *street name.* Instead of a formal certificate, these investors receive only a computer printout or similar statement showing what securities are being held for them. In addition to holding the securities, the brokerage house will forward all dividends, interest, annual reports, and voting material to their clients. When you wish to sell all or a portion of these securities, a phone call to the broker holding them in the street name is all that is required.

Securities held by brokers are either put in a bank vault or are deposited with the Depository Trust Company or other approved clearing agency. In either case, they are insured by the Security Investors Protection Corporation (SIPC) for up to $500,000.

BUYING STOCKS ON MARGIN

Buying stocks on margin means making a down payment of at least the margin percentage specified by the Federal Reserve Board (Regulation T) and borrowing the remainder from a stockbroker, banker, or other source. If the margin requirement is 60 percent, you must put down at least 60 percent of the cost of the stock plus commissions and borrow the remaining 40 percent. As we saw in Chapter 1, margin buying is simply using leverage to increase the risk or dispersion of possible returns on an investment. When prices rise, margin buying is likely to increase your rate of return over the one you would have gotten had you paid cash for the whole investment. On the other hand, when prices fall, margin buying will increase your rate of loss. (Strictly speaking, if your investment does not grow faster than the interest rate on the funds you borrowed, your investment could appreciate and you still might make a lower rate of return than if you had paid all of it and borrowed nothing.

If your investment grows at a faster rate, say, 18 percent, than the rate on your borrowings, say, 12 percent, then margining will have increased your overall rate of return.)

The most common source of loans to individuals wishing to buy securities on margin is from brokerage firms. Both full-service and discount brokerage companies lend money to qualified clients at rates generally 1 to 2 percent above the *prime rate* (the interest rate charged by banks to their best corporate customers) or above the *brokers' call rate* (the interest charged by banks to brokerage houses that borrow using stocks and other securities as collateral). Larger loans are usually made at lower rates of interest. To cover their loans, these companies hold the securities you purchase in their own name (i.e., they hold your securities in street name); thus they can negotiate (sell) them immediately if you default on your loan.

To further secure their loans, there is a *maintenance margin requirement* of 25 percent or more. Your net equity must be at least 25 percent of the amount you have borrowed; it might have to be more if the brokerage house sets higher requirements. Your *net equity* is the current sale value minus the borrowed balance. This figure divided by the borrowed balance must be at least 25 percent.

Let's take a specific example. Suppose you bought 100 shares of XYZ at $118 per share plus a $200 broker's fee. Your initial investment would be $12,000. If the margin requirement were 60 percent, you would have to put

Table 3.1   The Increase in Risk Resulting from Buying Stocks on Margin

	60 Percent Margin Purchase	100 Percent Margin or No Borrowing
Initial investment (100 shares at $118/share + $200 commission):		
Cash outlay	$ 7,280	$12,000
Borrowed funds (margined)	4,720	0
Initial purchase	$12,000	$12,000
Sale after 1 year with gain (100 shares at $150 per share):		
Gross receipts:	$15,000	$15,000
Commission to sell	− 250	− 250
Interest on loan	− 700	− 0
Repayment of loan principal	−4,720	− 0
Income tax liability	− 688*	− 688
Tax deduction for interest paid	+ 175†	0
Net receipts	$ 8,817	$14,062
Rate of return on initial cash outlay	21%‡	17%§

The sale price adjusted for commissions is $15,000 − $250, or $14,750. The purchase adjusted for commissions is $11,800 plus $200, or $12,000. The capital gain is $14,750 − $12,000, or $2750. Assuming a marginal tax rate of 25 percent (and no capital gains exclusion), the capital gains tax would be $687.50 or $688.
†*The $700 paid in interest is deductible for income tax purposes. If your marginal tax rate is 25 percent, and if you already itemize your deductions, this additional interest deduction reduces your tax liability by $175.*
‡*7280(1 + r)^1 = 8817, so r = 0.2111.*
§*12,000(1 + r)^1 = 14,062, so r = 0.1718.*

up at least $7280 in cash (60 percent of $11,800 plus $200 for commissions) and could borrow $4720 (see Table 3.1). At that time, the ratio of your net equity to borrowing well exceeds the 25 percent maintenance margin. Thus $11,800 minus $4720 equals $7080 divided by $4720 equals 150 percent, which is greater than the 25 percent requirement.

However, if XYZ stock fell below $59 per share, you would violate the maintenance margin. At $59 per share, the ratio of net equity ($5900 minus $4720) to your borrowed balance ($4720) would be exactly 25 percent. But at $52 per share, the ratio would be only 10.2 percent. In this case, if you did not immediately pay off part of your loan (i.e., reduce your borrowed balance), the broker would sell some of your stock and use the proceeds to pay off part of your loan for you in order to bring this ratio back above 25 percent. For example, if the broker sold 60 shares, it would reduce your debt by $3120 ($52 times 60 shares), leaving the new debt level at $1600 (ignoring broker charges for this sale). The new ratio of net equity to borrowing would rise to 30 percent, which is above the maintenance margin.

Table 3.1 also shows that the rate of return on your initial cash investment is higher if the investment is made on margin and *if* the stock appreciates. (In this case, the price is assumed to rise to $150 per share.) After adjustments are made for the broker's fees, the cost of interest on borrowed money, repayment of the loan principal, capital gains (income) taxes, and interest deductions for income taxes paid, the rate of return on the margined investment is 21 percent, compared to only 17 percent for the investment bought completely with cash.

The table does not show the effect of buying at the margin in the case of sale after a decline in price—in other words, in the case of a capital loss. However, as we have seen before, the percentage rate of loss would be much greater for such a leveraged or margined investment.

THE ALL-IN-ONE CENTRAL ASSET ACCOUNT

In 1977, Merrill Lynch introduced a new type of account for those people who wanted combined checking and brokerage services. They called it a Cash Management Account or simply a CMA. The idea was so innovative and so popular that other brokerage companies, large banks, and large mutual funds were forced to develop similar services that have come to be known generically as *central asset accounts* or *CAAs*. (Most investors still refer to them as CMAs, even though CMA is a Merrill Lynch trademark. It is like asking for a Kleenex or a Dixie cup instead of a facial tissue or a paper cup.) Dean Witter calls its CAA an Active Asset Account; E. F. Hutton calls it an Asset Management Account; Fidelity Investments calls it an Ultra Service Account; Chase Manhattan Bank calls it a Universal Account; and Charles Schwab calls it a Schwab One Account.

Although central asset accounts vary greatly with respect to initial investments, minimum balances, and annual fees, all offer the following in one account with one neat monthly statement:

¶ A money market mutual fund with check writing or with an interest-bearing checking account
¶ A brokerage account for stocks, bonds, and selected mutual funds

¶ A margin account for borrowing against securities
   you own
¶ A debit card such as VISA, MasterCard, or
   American Express

Others have added features, such as access to automatic
teller machines (ATMs), commission-free traveler's
checks, and expense analysis of checks written and
coded for medical bills, mortgage payments, contri-
butions, etc.

The principal advantages of a CAA are increased
portfolio efficiency and ease of personal portfolio
management. Instead of several monthly statements,
you get one comprehensive summary statement. Deposits, dividends, and interest on (say) bonds are automatically swept into an interest-bearing checking account. Access to your financial investments is
available (for some CAAs) 24 hours a day. Funds can
be easily withdrawn by check, by wire, by phone, by
ATM, or by, for example, a VISA debit card. Loans
can be made automatically; i.e., securities can be margined at rates far less than the typical credit-card–
cash-advance rate.

So why doesn't everyone have a CAA? To dis-
suade small accounts, most CAAs require a minimum
initial investment of, say, $20,000. They also impose
an annual service fee of, say, $50. Some require that a
minimum balance (e.g., $5000) be left in the account,
although most that do require a minimum balance do

not enforce the requirement unless you abuse it and are below the minimum for several months at a time.

Although similar, all CAAs are not alike. It pays to shop and compare the services you desire and their costs. If you have no stocks or bonds, a simple money market mutual fund might be preferable to a CAA. The VISA debit card connected to a Merrill Lynch CMA is convenient because it gives you borrowing power up to the marginable amount of securities you have, but it is more problematic when you want to refuse payment on defective goods purchased with a credit card. Most people like their checks returned; Merrill Lynch's CMA does not return checks, whereas Fidelity's USA does. Moreover, as a self-directed investor, why pay full-service fees to buy and sell stocks in a Merrill Lynch CMA when you could do so for half the commissions in a Schwab One or a Fidelity USA account? (One nice feature with the Merrill Lynch CMA is that the minimum balance need be only $1, whereas the Fidelity USA requires a minimum balance of $5000.) Finally, many older investors want to hold their securities themselves in certificate form. They do not like the idea of leaving them in a street name, even in an insured CAA account.

Most middle- and upper-income people find the advantages of a CAA account to outweigh their costs. Even if you do not use all the standard CAA features, such as margining, you should consider such an account as a repository for idle funds, i.e., as an account where you can easily manage your cash.

POINTS TO REMEMBER

¶ Common stocks are equities in corporations; bonds are debts of corporations, governments, and government agencies; and preferred stocks are a marriage of the two.

¶ Returns on securities are not subject to Social Security taxes because they are considered or counted as "unearned income."

¶ Brokers are middlemen in the capital market, a market that is so dispersed and complicated that middlemen are virtually indispensable.

¶ The typical commission on stocks is about 2 percent of the value purchased; discount brokers charge about half as much.

¶ Brokers are convenient sources of market information; they provide other services, including lending money to buy securities on margin.

¶ Margining enhances risk and hence the chance for higher and lower rates of return. It is easily done, particularly if the securities are kept in a central asset account.

4

BONDS AND FIXED-INCOME SECURITIES

Like stocks, bonds are held by individuals mainly for two reasons: (1) the expectation of interest income, and (2) the expectation of appreciation in the bond's market value.[1] In addition, bonds are often considered safer investments when market values of alternative investments are expected to fall or to continue falling. This is comparable to the speculative motive for holding cash; i.e., the demand for holding cash increases as more people expect interest rates to rise and hence the prices of fixed-income securities to fall.

As we have seen before, the interest paid on bonds is a form of so-called unearned income. As such, it is exempt from Social Security taxes. Interest also may be exempt from federal and/or from state and local taxes for specially designated bonds. These tax-exempt bonds will be discussed later in this chapter.

Like the capital gains on stocks, the (long-term) capital gains realized on bonds used to be taxed at only 40 percent of the marginal tax rate. This was the same as saying that 60 percent of the long-term gain went tax-free as far as federal income taxes are concerned. Currently, both long- and short-term capital gains on all bonds, even tax-exempt municipals, are taxed at ordinary income tax rates.

PURCHASING BONDS

Newly issued U.S. government bonds can be purchased, with no broker's fees or commissions, directly from the Treasury or from a Federal Reserve Bank. If you choose instead to buy through a broker or a commercial bank, there is a charge of about $60 for each bond, whether it is a $1000 bond, a $10,000 bond, or a $100,000 bond. Treasury bonds and notes are no longer issued as certificates. Instead, they are issued in *book-entry form,* meaning that you get a simple receipt, like a bank statement, with an account number. Federal agency bonds and municipal bonds currently issued by state and local governments also can be purchased through banks or brokers. Newly issued corporate bonds are generally purchased from an *underwriter,* usually a large bank or brokerage firm acting as an intermediary between the large borrower, the corporation, and the many small lenders, the individual investors. The underwriter takes the bonds and guarantees the corporation a certain amount of money for them. Then the underwriter advertises, promotes, and otherwise "markets" the bonds to the general public. The supply and demand for newly issued securities constitutes the *primary bond market.*

The *secondary bond market* is formed by individuals and corporations wishing to trade previously issued bonds. These securities are bought and sold (demanded and supplied) in established markets, such as the New

York Stock Exchange, as well as in the over-the-counter market. Large brokerage firms are the intermediaries through which most individuals enter these secondary markets. Therefore, if you want to buy a previously issued bond, you usually do so through a broker, such as Merrill Lynch, Dean Witter, or A. G. Edwards.

BOND RATINGS

It would be difficult for an individual to evaluate a company's or even a local government's ability to honor its bond or debt obligations. Such an evaluation would involve a careful examination of the company's financial statements (income statements and balance sheets) and a projection and comparison of revenues and expenditures. It would be even more difficult to repeat such evaluations for a wide range of companies and then to derive a relative index of the degree of risk inherent in their bonds.

Fortunately, the individual investor need not make such evaluations. Several advisory services publish ratings that rank bonds from the best quality to the worst. The best-known services are Moody's and Standard & Poor's; their ratings may be obtained from brokers and most large libraries.

The Standard & Poor's *Bond Guide* is a monthly rating of about 6500 bonds, including 5600 domestic and Canadian corporate bonds, over 275 foreign bonds, and over 640 convertible bonds. It is compiled by a 325-member analytical staff and is commonly known as the "blue list" because of its blue cover. As you can see below, the bond ratings published by Moody's and Standard & Poor's are very similar. The best bonds, the least risky ones, are rated Aaa or AAA. These triple-A bonds are issued by very large, very stable corporations or by governments with good past performance and excellent future projections for being able to honor their bonds.

Bond Ratings Published by Moody's and Standard & Poor's

Moody's	Aaa	Aa	A	Baa	Ba	B	Caa	Ca	C	
Standard & Poor's	AAA	AA	A	BBB	BB	B	CCC	CC	C	D

There is a tendency toward the higher ratings for both Moody's and Standard & Poor's. Indeed, Moody's gives no D's, and neither service gives an F. There are very few large, well-known bond issues with ratings lower than Baa. This reflects, in part, the fact that bonds—even poorer ones—are legal debt obligations of companies and governments and are relatively safe investments.

BUYING BONDS FOR CASH

The brokers' fees to buy and sell bonds are generally lower than for stocks of comparable value. Unlike stock commissions, however, which are based on the dollar amount of the transaction, bond commissions are based on the number of bonds traded, not on their market value or face value. In other words, there is a fee per bond regardless of the size of the bond. One of the larger brokerage firms charges the following rates:

1 to 5 bonds:	$5 per bond
6 to 10 bonds:	$4 per bond
11 or more bonds:	$3 per bond

Thus to sell three $1000 XYZ bonds would cost you $15 in commissions or one-half of 1 percent of their value. To sell three $10,000 XYZ bonds would cost the same dollar amount but be only one-twentieth of 1 percent. Compare these transactions costs to the average 2 percent stock commissions of most full-service brokers.

BUYING BONDS ON MARGIN

Because bonds are thought to be safer investments, the Federal Reserve Board's margin requirement (the minimum amount required to be paid as a down payment) is much more liberal for bonds than for stocks. You can borrow money to buy bonds with only 10 percent down for government bonds and 30 percent down for corporate bonds. By comparison, the Federal Reserve Board currently requires 50 percent down for all stocks. (The interest you pay on margin debt, or any debt to buy or carry investments, is tax deductible unless the debt is incurred to purchase tax-exempt municipal securities.) If you want to increase your risk through leverage, bonds provide a better alternative than stocks because of this difference in government regulations. In subsequent discussions of options and commodity futures, we shall see how leverage can be increased still further.

ESTIMATING BOND VALUES

As we have already seen, a bond is a claim on money, a claim based on the promise of payment by the corporation (or government) issuing it. It is a claim on the principal originally lent to the corporation plus a series of additional claims on money for interest. The interest is the compensation for having lent the corporation the principal amount and for the risk involved in holding its bond.

Like a stock, a bond is valuable precisely because it is a claim on assets. Although corporations (and governments) that issue bonds are the primary source of supply, current bondholders willing to part with their bonds for a price are the major suppliers in the secondary bond market. The higher the price offered for a particular bond (say, a $1000, 9 percent January/July bond, with 5 years until maturity), the more such bonds will be offered for sale, i.e., supplied. The demand for bonds comes mostly from those who want a safe investment with a fixed periodic return, e.g., payable every January and July. Bonds are generally safer than stocks precisely because they are legal obligations of the corporation (or government) that issued them. Remember, in the event of bankruptcy, bondholders must be paid off before anything is distributed to the stockholders.

Together, the supply and demand for a particular bond determine its market price. Since both the supply and the demand can change at any time, the market price is subject to fluctuation even though the promises made in the bond itself remain unchanged. For example, if interest rates in the economy fall, the fixed rate specified in a bond will look more attractive. In other words, with interest rates down, the 9 percent (or the $45 paid in January and in July on the bond mentioned earlier) looks better. The demand for the bond is likely to increase, and if supply remains the same, the bond's price will increase as well.

From the point of view of an investor (even one who does not plan to keep bonds until they mature), bonds are valuable because of (1) their expected interest promised at periodic intervals and (2) the expected appreciation in their market price. These two factors combined give the *expected yield* or *expected return* on the bond.

Let's take a specific example. Consider a highly rated, newly issued 5-year $1000 bond bearing an interest rate of 9 percent. Unlike the bond mentioned earlier, assume this bond pays the interest of $90 in a lump sum once each year (the stated interest rate of 9 percent times the face value of $1000) and when the bond matures after 5 years, the bondholder also can expect to receive the face value of $1000. Total expected returns are $1450— $450 from interest (5 years × $90 per year) plus the $1000 face value.

The value of this bond is not $1450, however. This

stream of expected returns takes place over a period of time; the stream is time-dimensioned and must be adjusted if its total value is to be measured at one point in time, such as the present. Each return received in the future must be discounted to calculate its value as of today.

Suppose you could earn 10 percent on a money market mutual fund, a certificate of deposit, or some other similarly low-risk asset. Let's use 10 percent to discount the expected returns on our high-quality 5-year bond. The first $90 of expected bond interest would be worth $81.82 if paid today instead of 1 year from today, because if you had $81.82 today and could earn 10 percent on it, it would grow to exactly $90 by the end of the year. The present value equals the future value divided by 1 plus the discount rate: $81.82 = $90/1.1.

The second $90 of expected bond interest would have to be discounted two times, since it would be received 2 years from now. Thus $90 divided by 1.1 and divided again by 1.1 equals $74.38. The third $90 would have to be discounted three times: $90 divided by 1.1^3 equals $67.62. Thus the present value of $90 paid 3 years from now is only $67.62, assuming a time rate of discount of 10 percent. Check this by asking yourself, "If I had $67.62 today and could earn 10 percent on it, how much would it be worth at the end of 3 years?" After 1 year, it would be worth $74.38, or $67.62 times 1.10; after 2 years, it would be worth $81.82, or $74.38 times 1.10; and after 3 years, it would be worth $90, or $81.82 times 1.10.

In order to estimate the present value of the entire stream of returns on this bond, we would have to solve the following equation:

$$\text{Present value} = \frac{\$90}{1.1} + \frac{\$90}{1.1^2} + \frac{\$90}{1.1^3} + \frac{\$90}{1.1^4} + \frac{\$90}{1.1^5} + \frac{\$1000}{1.1^5}$$

$$= \$81.82 + 74.38 + \$67.62 + \$61.47$$

$$+ \$55.88 + \$620.92$$

$$= \$962.09$$

The present value of this bond, discounting the expected returns for time, is $962.09.

Go back over this example and note these important points:

1. The interest rate stated on the bond, 9 percent, was the rate multiplied by the face value to get the expected returns. This interest rate is not the same as the time rate of discount, 10 percent. Of course, these two rates could be the same, but they usually are not.
2. The present value ($962.09) and the face value ($1000) are not the same.
3. The present value of the bond varies inversely with the rate used as a discount factor. Had we used 12 percent, the present value would have been only $891.84. In other words, increasing our discount factor from 10 to 12 percent causes the present value to fall from $962.09 to $891.84, for a decline of 7.3 percent.

4. The sum of the expected returns, including the maturity value, has little meaning or relevance.
5. The analysis is the same for a 20-year, 9 percent, $1000 bond with 5 years left until maturity as for a newly issued 5-year, 9 percent, $1000 bond.
6. The discount factor of 10 percent was chosen to represent the opportunity cost of not getting the expected returns until specific times in the future. It reflected the going market rate of interest on very safe alternative financial assets. However, that rate of 10 percent is subjective; there is no universally agreed upon time rate of discount.
7. A rise in the interest rate will cause a smaller fall in the value of a short-term bond compared with a long-term bond. If the interest rate rises from 10 to 12 percent, a $1000, 9 percent, 1-year bond will fall in present value (*PV*) from $990.91 to $973.21, or only 1.79 percent. To see this, discount the bond at 10 percent:

$$PV = \frac{\$90}{1.10} + \frac{\$1000}{1.10} = \$81.82 + \$909.09 = \$990.91$$

Then discount the bond at 12 percent:

$$PV = \frac{\$90}{1.12} + \frac{\$1000}{1.12} = \$80.36 + \$892.86 = \$973.22$$

The difference is $990.91 - $973.22 = $17.69

And $$\frac{\$17.69}{\$990.91} = 1.79 \text{ percent}$$

However, if the interest rate rises from 10 to 12 percent on a 5-year bond ($1000 at 9 percent), the bond will fall in value from $962.09 to $891.84, or 7.3 percent. Similarly, a fall in the interest rate will cause a greater rise in the value of a long-term bond than it will in the value of a short-term bond.

A good understanding of these points allows us to clear up much of the confusion surrounding bonds and their values. Let's use the example to answer some commonly asked questions:

1. *Why is a rise in prevailing market interest rates usually followed by a fall in bond prices?* Such a rise leads investors to increase their time discount rates, thereby lowering present values, making bonds less attractive, and lowering the demand for them. At lower prices, the bond yield rises back toward competitive levels.

2. *If two bonds have identical face values, interest rates, and time left until maturity, why might they still differ in price?* One answer is that one bond might be more risky than the other. Investors not only discount for time but also for risk. For the more risky bond (issued, say, by the Hooker Chemical Company during the Love Canal disaster), investors are likely to use a higher discount rate and arrive at a lower present value.

3. *Why do some bonds sell for less than their face value while others sell for more?* If the stated

interest rate on a bond is less than the prevailing market discount rate, as was the case in our example, the present value ($962.09) will be less than its face value ($1000), and the bond will "sell at a discount." If the stated interest rate on the bond is higher than the prevailing market discount rate, the present value would exceed $1000, and the bond would "sell at a premium."

4. *How is the yield on a bond calculated?* Yields are difficult to calculate by hand and are usually done with programmable electronic calculators. Here is a simple formula for approximating the yield on a bond held to maturity:

$$\text{Estimated yield if held to maturity} = \frac{ER + [(FV - P)/n]}{(P + FV)/2}$$

where ER = annual expected interest payment in dollars
FV = face value of bond, usually $1000
P = price of the bond
n = number of years until maturity.

Consider our 5-year, $1000 bond bearing an interest rate of 9 percent. If the current market price were $1040, the bond would be selling at a premium, and the yield would be 8.04 percent. If the market price were $926, the bond would be selling at a discount, and the yield would be estimated at 10.88 percent. (Actual yields would be exactly 8 and 11 percent, respectively.)

INVESTING IN TAX-EXEMPT BONDS

Bonds issued by state and local governments and their agencies are called *municipal bonds* or *munis*. Municipal bonds are categorized as either *general-obligation bonds* or *revenue bonds*. The former are secured by the full faith, credit, and taxing power of the issuer; the latter are secured by the revenue, such as tolls and rents, charged by the project financed by the bonds. Since the early 1980s, private-purpose revenue bonds have been largely responsible for the dramatic growth in the number of municipal bonds. The proceeds of these private-purpose issues have been used to finance pollution-control facilities, sports facilities and convention centers, airport facilities, irrigation projects, and industrial parks.

While municipal bonds are issued by governments or related authorities, they differ from Treasury bonds in several ways. There are over 50,000 different tax-exempt issuers and over 1 million different tax-exempt securities, mainly owing to the large number of relatively small issues by private-purpose projects. As a result, many municipal bonds are not traded in the national market and may be very thinly traded (if at all) in local markets.

Interest received on municipal bonds is exempt from federal income tax, although it must be declared on Form 1040 and even though it does count as income when making the computation to determine if part or all of Social Security benefits are to be taxed. Municipal bond interest is also typically exempt from state and local income taxes in the locale in which they were issued. Thus interest on Arizona Salt River Bonds is not taxed to residents of Arizona by the state of Arizona, but it is taxed to residents of New York by the state of New York. Historically, this income tax exemption has been given to allow state and local governments to issue debt at below competitive market rates. (The tax-exempt status is a subsidy to state and local governments by the federal government, a subsidy repaid in kind by state and local governments who exempt Treasury bill interest from their income taxes.) Other things being equal, tax-exempt bonds are preferable to bonds whose interest is taxed. However, other things are not always equal. When tax-exempt bonds pay less interest, their yields should be compared on a taxable-equivalent basis.

To compute a taxable-equivalent yield for residents of areas with no state or local income tax, divide the tax-exempt yield by 1 minus the investor's marginal tax rate. Thus, if you are in the 35 percent federal income tax bracket, a 10 percent tax-exempt municipal bond would have a taxable-equivalent yield of

$$\frac{0.10}{1 - 0.35} \quad \text{or 15.38 percent}$$

In other words, if you earned 15.38 percent before taxes and were in the 35 percent tax bracket, after taxes you would have a yield of 10 percent. So 10 percent tax-exempt is equivalent to 15.38 percent taxable.

For residents of areas with state and local income taxes, these taxes can be deducted from taxable income when computing federal income taxes. In this case, the formula for the taxable-equivalent yield becomes

Taxable-equivalent yield

$$= \frac{\text{tax-exempt yield}}{1 - MFTR - MSTR + (MFTR \times MSTR)}$$

where $MFTR$ = marginal *federal* tax rate
$MSTR$ = marginal *state* tax rate

Marginal in these terms is a synonym for *extra*; in this case, it refers to the tax rate applied to an extra dollar's worth of income. For progressive taxes, such as federal and most state income taxes, the marginal tax rate rises as taxable income increases; hence the marginal tax rate is greater than the average tax rate. Thus if you are in the 35 percent federal income tax bracket and in the 12 percent state (and local) income tax bracket, a 10 percent tax-exempt municipal bond would have a taxable equivalent yield of

$$\frac{0.10}{1 - 0.35 - 0.12 + (0.35 \times 0.12)} \text{ or } 17.48 \text{ percent}$$

What this means is that a 10 percent tax-free or tax-exempt bond is worth the same as a 17.48 percent taxable bond for a person in those tax brackets. You can check this. Suppose you had invested $10,000 in a 17.48 percent corporate bond whose interest was fully taxable. In 1 year, you would have received $1748 in interest before taxes. Then you would have to pay state income taxes of $210, that is, 12 percent times $1748. As a result of owning this bond, your federal taxable income would have been $1748 higher, but because you had to pay $210 more in state income taxes (a deduction, assuming you itemize your deductions), it would only be a net of $1538 higher. This would cause you to pay $538 in federal income taxes as a result of owning the bond. Thus you received $1748 in taxable interest, paid $538 in federal income taxes and $210 in state income taxes, and ended up with $1000 in after-tax interest. On your $10,000 investment, this is equal to a tax-exempt yield of 10 percent. In other words, you would be indifferent to receiving $1748 in taxable interest or $1000 in tax-exempt interest.

Municipal bonds are attractive for other reasons besides their tax-exempt status. For one thing, as a group, they are considered to be safe investments, although less safe than federal government bonds. Moreover, even where occasional defaults do occur, most municipal governments eventually satisfy their obligations in full. Some municipal bonds offer floating rates that fluctuate weekly with interest rates on key Treasury issues; investors may find this feature attractive because it causes these bonds to trade fairly close to their original issue price and thereby precludes a large decline in market value if interest rates in general should suddenly rise. (Of course, floating rates also preclude large capital gains if interest rates in general should suddenly fall causing the market value of the bonds to rise above what you paid for them.) Still other municipal bonds attract investors with guarantees by the municipality to repurchase the bonds at their face value after, say, 5 years. These are sometimes called *put bonds* or *option bonds*.

Municipal bonds are also marketable, at least for the

larger issues. They can be rather easily bought and sold by investors prior to maturity. The secondary market for municipals provides a place to buy and sell issues maturing from next month to 50 years from now. One drawback, however, is that the usual minimum denomination is $5000. This restricts many small investors, who might instead look to tax-exempt money market mutual funds. These funds often package municipal bonds by state to come up with, say, the California Fund. Investors can purchase as little as $1000 of shares in this fund, and if they are residents of California, the dividends they earn (from interest the California Fund earns on the California municipal bonds in its portfolio) are completely tax exempt.

DEEP-DISCOUNT BONDS

As an alternative to the traditional fixed-rate long-term bond, some bonds are issued with very low coupon rates (the interest rate, stated on the bond, which when multiplied by the face value of the bond gives the annual dollar interest paid). In the extreme, the coupon interest rate can be zero, meaning no interest at all is paid. The only thing left is a promise to pay the face value at a specific time, e.g., 20 years, in the future. For such *zeros,* the expected annual returns are zero, so their present value is simply their future (face) value discounted for time, risk, and inflation. For example, if we discount a $100,000 zero-coupon bond maturing in 20 years at 10 percent, its present value would be

$$\text{Present value} = \frac{FV}{(1 + d)^t} = \frac{\$100,000}{1.1^{20}} = \$14,864$$

where FV = future value or face
value of the bond,
in this case $100,000

d = discount rate for time,
risk, and inflation,
in this case 10 percent

t = time to maturity,
in this case 20 years

Of course, every investor would not discount this particular bond for time, risk, and inflation at exactly 10 percent. For those who would discount at a lower rate, the present value would be higher (e.g., at 8 percent, it would be $21,454); for those who would discount at a higher rate, the present value would be lower (e.g., at 12 percent, it would be $10,367). However, if those who demand and those who supply these bonds generally employ a 10 percent discount rate, this zero-coupon bond will be found trading in the market at around $14,864.

Zero-coupon bonds may be ideal investments for some individuals. Unlike conventional bonds, they are not likely to be called in by the borrower earlier than their maturity date. Then too, there is no problem with handling interest payments and deciding where to reinvest them, because there are no interest payments. Zeros provide a simple way to amass a particular amount of money at a future point in time.

The biggest disadvantage with investing in zero-coupon bonds is that even though no interest is received, the Internal Revenue Service taxes the investor as though interest had been received on a straight-line basis. This means that interest must be computed, tax forms must be completed, and taxes must be paid every year, instead of just when the bond is sold and a capital gain realized. This disadvantage is avoided by foreign investors (who pay no U.S. income taxes) and by those who put zeros in IRA or other tax-deferred retirement accounts. Consequently, zeros and other deep-discount bonds are not suitable for most investors, particularly those who are retired and need a steady source of income.

CONVERTIBLE SECURITIES

A *convertible bond* is a corporate bond that can be exchanged for shares of common stock of the same company. The exact number of shares of stock for which the bond can be exchanged is specified in the bond at the time it is first issued. Naturally, the market value of this specified number of shares is less than the cost of the bond. If the price of the common stock increases, the value of these shares could exceed the purchase price of the bond, meaning an appreciation in its value. If the bond is sold or if it is converted into common stock, this appreciation becomes a capital gain.

Suppose the XYZ Company issues a $1000, 6 percent, 5-year convertible bond that can be exchanged for 20 shares of XYZ common stock currently selling at $45 per share. Suppose, too, that the bond is currently selling *at par,* i.e., for $1000. No rational investor will exercise the conversion privilege, because to do so would yield only 20 shares worth $900.

If the price of the common stock rises to over $50 per share, an investor could convert to common stock with a value of over $1000. If it rose to $55, for example, the 20 shares would be worth $1100, and the investor could then sell these and reap a $100 capital gain. (Of course, these computations ignore transactions costs, including broker's fees.)

The convertible feature makes a bond more attractive because it gives an investor a chance for greater appreciation than would an ordinary bond. Because of this benefit, however, convertible bonds usually bear lower rates of interest. If bond *A* and bond *C* are both selling for $1000 and bond *C* is convertible, it is likely that bond *C*'s interest rate (and hence its expected return) is lower, usually about a third lower than nonconvertible bond *A*.

An easier way to see the value of a bond's being convertible is to compare the price of a convertible bond with the price of a regular bond having the same maturity, interest rate, and business risk. The convertible bond will have a higher market price; in other words, there will be a premium for its being convertible. Investment experts do not generally recommend a convertible bond when its premium is more than 10 percent above the price at which it would sell if it were an ordinary bond.

When the market is falling, the prices of convertible

bonds also tend to fall, although not nearly as sharply as the prices of their underlying common stock, because convertible bonds are often held as a hedge against sharp downward swings in the securities market.

The same is true for preferred stock that may be converted into a specified number of shares of common stock. Convertible preferred stock promises fixed dividends in periods of market decline and a chance for appreciation when the prices of common stock increase rapidly.

BUYING AND SELLING MORTGAGES

Like a bond, a mortgage is an IOU. However, instead of yielding a stream of interest payments (e.g., $50 semiannually over 20 years for a 10 percent $1000 bond) and then the principal (in this case, $1000), a mortgage yields a stream of amortization payments. These include both interest and principal. To *amortize* a debt, means to pay its interest and a portion of its principal each period until it is paid off. Traditionally, mortgage payments have been constant amounts with higher portions of interest in earlier payments and lower portions in later ones. Beginning in the 1980s, traditional mortgages were modified with adjustable rates and other variations. In this discussion, however, we shall concentrate on typical fixed-rate mortgages with constant periodic payments.

We saw that bonds are relatively safe investments because they are debts of corporations, state and local governments, or the federal government. Mortgages are (usually) debts of individuals, but their safety is enhanced because they are secured by real property, such as a house or an apartment building or vacant land, which is pledged in case the borrower defaults.

Whereas most corporate bonds that are likely to be held by individuals have face values of $1000, and whereas most municipal bonds have face values of $5000, mortgages are not written in any standard amounts. Moreover, because they are not issued for standard amounts, and because they are not (and cannot be easily) rated for risk, they are not as widely traded in secondary markets. There is no "blue list" for mortgages as there is for the most widely traded bonds. This makes buying and selling mortgages more difficult; hence as an investment, mortgages are more illiquid.

Buying and selling mortgages can be very profitable for financially sophisticated investors. It is not uncommon for individuals to purchase a mortgage at such a large discount from its current balance that the investment yields a 20 to 25 percent rate of return. However, even less sophisticated investors with portfolios as small as $100,000 might consider taking a mortgage if the circumstances are right. For example, you might take a 5-year second mortgage for $10,000 at, say, 11 percent on a home purchased by a son or daughter. Not only might you be helping your child, but you would be getting almost twice as much as you would on an ordinary passbook savings account.

If you decide to invest in a mortgage, here are some tips to ensure a better rate of return:

1. *Only consider mortgages on real estate in your area.* You should be able to examine the property and feel comfortable that its market value fully secures the mortgage. You should be able to easily review recorded deeds, mortgages, and judgments that concern this property or you should be able to easily hire an attorney to do this for you. There are enough mortgage opportunities within 10 miles to satisfy even the biggest investors. (Obviously, a mortgage or loan to a son or daughter living out of the area may be the exception to this rule.)

2. *Do not purchase mortgages that will not be paid off in less than 5 years,* unless you are willing to wait longer for your money. Remember, unlike stocks and bonds, mortgages held by individuals are very illiquid assets. It will not be easy to sell or trade a mortgage, except at a high discount off its present value. Therefore, unless you are willing to suffer a capital loss, be prepared to hold the mortgage until maturity.

Professionals who advertise to buy mortgages often discount them to yield rates of return of 20 to 25 percent. To get a better feel for this, let's consider a specific example. Suppose you held a 10 percent mortgage that was originally for $80,000 to be repaid over 20 years in monthly installments of $772. Furthermore, suppose that 8 years have passed since the mortgage was begun; the current balance owed is $64,599. If you needed to sell this mortgage, a sophisticated mortgage buyer might offer you, say, $36,400. This mortgage buyer knows that the remaining 144 monthly payments of $772 each will yield a 10 percent rate of return if he or she pays the balance of $64,599. However, the payments will yield about 24 percent if he or she pays only $36,400. You can check this by solving the following equation for r, the annual rate of return:

$$36{,}400 = \frac{772}{1 + r/12} + \frac{772}{(1 + r/12)^2} + \cdots + \frac{772}{(1 + r/12)^{144}}$$

$$= 772 \times \frac{1 - 1/(1 + r/12)^{144}}{r/12}$$

r = approximately 0.24, or 24 percent per year

Test yourself. If the mortgage buyer wanted an 18 percent rate of return, what would he or she pay? In this case,

$$\text{Present value} = \frac{772}{1 + 0.18/12} + \frac{772}{(1 + 0.18/12)^2} + \cdots +$$

$$\frac{772}{(1 + 0.18/12)^{144}}$$

$$= 772 \times \frac{1 - 1/(1 + 0.18/12)^{144}}{0.18/12}$$

$$= \$45{,}436$$

Therefore, the buyer would be willing to pay $45,436 for your mortgage that has 144 more monthly payments of $772 each.

3. *For new mortgages, structure the mortgage to suit your preferences.* If monthly payments are bothersome, have the mortgage written so that payments are made quarterly, semiannually, or annually.

To reduce the problem with mortgage illiquidity, have the mortgage written to include a *balloon payment* at the end of, say, 3 years. For a new $80,000, 20-year, 10-percent mortgage, this would mean the borrower would pay $772 each month for 36 months and then have to pay a big final payment of $75,598. After 36 months, the borrower would have to either pay this mortgage off, refinance it with some other party, or refinance it with you. For a mortgage holder, a balloon payment makes this very illiquid asset more liquid because it is self-liquidating after 36 months. In the preceding example, if the balloon payment were set at the end of 8 years, you would get $64,599, whereas if there were no balloon payment and you had to sell the mortgage quickly, you might get only $30,000 to $40,000 from a professional mortgage broker.

4. *Contact a good local lawyer who is actively engaged in real estate transactions.* Mortgages (and the notes that accompany them) are flexible legal documents with more clauses and pitfalls than the average investor can digest. You need a diligent attorney, preferably one who is familiar with the property that secures the mortgage. (A corporate attorney or one from a rather distant big-name legal firm is not likely to be suitable for this job.)

If local attorneys know that you are willing to lend money and take back a mortgage or that you are willing to buy a mortgage from someone else, they can often help their clients and you at the same time. They might have a client who needs to borrow for 2 or 3 years and is willing to pay above-market interest for the speed and convenience of a privately made mortgage. Instead of applying at several banks, submitting to credit checks, hiring a surveyor, hiring an appraiser, paying front-end mortgage fees (such as points), and going through all the financial transaction costs associated with procuring a bank mortgage, many borrowers will pay 2 to 5 percent above the current market rates. Thus, if bank mortgages are being made at 10 percent, some borrowers are willing to pay, say, 15 percent to borrow privately for the short term. (Of course, if borrowers want longer-term loans, the bank's transactions costs represent a smaller portion of the long-term finance cost, and bank loans would be more attractive.) Many times lawyers will include the cost of drawing and recording the mortgage in the fees they charge to the borrower, so that you, the lender, end up paying no transactions costs.

5. *Be careful when dealing with mortgage brokers.* Another source of mortgages for individuals looking to buy or sell is a mortgage broker. They trade first, second, and even third mortgages on the underlying real estate pledged as collateral to secure these loans. (In California, a second mortgage is called a *second-trust deed*.) Mortgage brokers are simply making a market in these investments; their profits are generated by buying mortgages at large discounts and selling them at near their principal balances. Where mortgage markets are thin (meaning there are few mortgages bought or sold), mortgage brokers can achieve a spread of 20 percent or more. Where there are greater numbers of mortgages traded

and where there is more competition, as in southern California, the spread is 6 to 10 percent.

There is no theoretical problem with the role of a legitimate mortgage broker, who is providing a service of bringing buyers (lenders) and sellers (borrowers) together. However, among the unregulated mortgage brokers, there are many rip-off artists. Therefore, the services of a competent attorney are necessary to ensure that the property exists, that its value exceeds the mortgage and prior mortgages by at least 20 percent, and that all the paperwork is properly completed. The risks of dealing with mortgage brokers can be reduced further by buying several smaller mortgages instead of one large one and by investigating and monitoring the properties yourself.

POINTS TO REMEMBER

¶ The commissions to buy and sell bonds are quite low and vary according to the number, not the value, of the bonds.

¶ The value of a bond is determined by discounting its expected returns, meaning the expected income from interest plus principal at maturity.

¶ The choice of "the" appropriate discount rate is subjective; as a result, some investors value the same bond more highly than others and are willing to bid more for it.

¶ Long-term bonds are more sensitive to changes in the interest rate than are short-term bonds.

¶ Tax-exempt bonds are usually only desirable for

those investors who are in high marginal tax brackets. It is foolish to beat the "tax man" only to end up with a lower after-tax return.

¶ Deep-discount bonds promise more capital gains than interest income; in the case of zero-coupon bonds, there is no interest at all.

¶ Convertible bonds and convertible preferred stock are not as popular with most investors, but they do offer some special features you might find attractive.

¶ Buying and selling mortgages can be an exciting and profitable way to invest, although in most cases such investments are better suited to sophisticated investors. Since mortgages are traded in a largely unregulated market, the services of a competent attorney are essential.

5

MUTUAL FUNDS, OPTIONS, AND FUTURES CONTRACTS

For many investors, even those who are philosophically and politically quite conservative, investments in stocks and bonds sometimes appear too tame or too "establishment." We have already seen that stereotyping these investments in this way is not accurate and that particular stocks and bonds, namely, the low-grade, high-yield ones, can be very speculative and exciting (win or lose). Regardless of how correct the ho-hum image of stocks and bonds is, however, other financial investments are attracting today's investors.

MUTUAL FUNDS

A *mutual fund* is a company that pools investment money from individuals (and institutional investors, such as pension funds, labor union accounts, and bank trust departments) and uses this money to buy securities from corporations, governments, and government agencies. As such, a mutual fund is a financial intermediary. Its liabilities are the shares it issues to individual investors. Its assets are the securities it has purchased in the market. This intermediary relationship is shown in Figure 5.1.

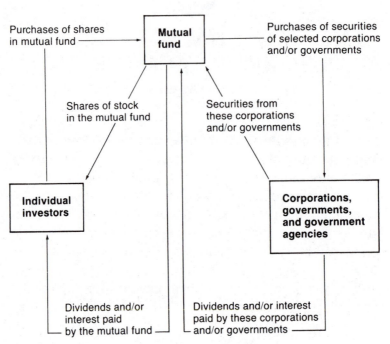

FIGURE 5.1 A mutual fund is a financial intermediary that pools the money of individual investors and uses it to buy a range of selected financial investments.

What Figure 5.1 does not show is how the mutual fund makes a profit. Very simply, before passing through any returns on the securities it holds, the fund charges a *management and expense fee,* which is typically 0.75 to 1.25 percent of its total assets. For a simple example, if a particular fund holds $1 million in government bonds that pay 10 percent per year, it might charge 1 percent ($10,000) as an annual management and expense fee.

The rest of the interest ($90,000) would be passed through to the mutual fund's shareholders, giving them an effective return of 9 percent. The managers of a mutual fund (presumably) try to select assets wisely to maximize the fund's earnings, since this promises to attract new investors and thereby generate even more assets. In addition, the larger the fund's total assets, the larger is its management income.

LOADS VS. NO-LOADS

In addition to management fees, some funds levy a sales charge at the time an investor first purchases shares. This sales charge is often referred to as a *front-end load*; it is typically 7 to 8½ percent of the entire payment. For example, if you pay $10,000 for American Capital Harbor Fund offered at $10 per share and having an 8½ percent loading charge, you will receive 1000 shares each with a net asset value (the total assets minus liabilities, and all divided by the number of shares) of $9.15. (If you immediately sold these 1000 shares, you would receive their combined net asset value of $9150.) The $850 sales charge is the commission going to the broker or to the mutual-fund salesperson who sells you these shares. Remember, a sales charge is distinct from, and paid in addition to, the management and advisory fees. The advantage of *load funds* is that you get the advice of a broker or salesperson. The disadvantage is that you must pay for it. (There is no significant difference in the average return on load funds compared to no-load funds.)

Mutual funds that do not levy load charges are called *no-load funds*. Their shares are sold directly to the individual investor with no broker or salesperson involved. With a no-load fund, you simply fill out a brief application (listing name, address, Social Security number, etc.) and send it, together with a check, directly to the mutual fund. The number of shares you receive is equal to the amount you send divided by the net asset value per share on the day your check is received. You could spend $10,000 today to buy 1000 shares of a no-load fund with a net asset value (*NAV*) of $10 per share and sell the same 1000 shares tomorrow to get back your entire $10,000 with no charges (loads) either coming or going. This assumes, of course, that the *NAV* does not change between the two days.

Some no-load funds do have *rear-end loads,* also called *exit charges* or *redemption fees*. These are designed to discourage investors from switching out soon after they get into a fund. Redemption fees are justified on the grounds that the fund cannot properly manage investment money put in and pulled out like a yo-yo. The typical redemption fee is 1 percent and is usually only charged to amounts withdrawn within the first 6 months after they were put in.

TYPES OF MUTUAL FUNDS

In Chapter 2 we discussed one type of mutual fund whose assets were short-term, high-grade IOUs of the federal government, large banks, and large blue-chip companies (commercial paper). Remember, these assets are known as *money market instruments,* and the funds are known as *money market mutual funds.* Now let's look at mutual funds that specialize in a host of other financial investments—some mild and some spicy. The classifications are rather arbitrary, and any specific fund may fit into one or more of these categories.

Stock funds are the most common mutual funds. Some concentrate on stocks with high dividends (*income funds*); these are particularly suitable for retired investors or for others who hold securities for the purpose of getting a steady stream of income.

Some stock funds concentrate on issues with the best chance of steady growth and hence the promise of future capital gains. These are called *growth funds.* If they are particularly aggressive in buying and selling, they are often referred to as *performance funds* or *aggressive growth funds.*

Other stock funds aim for both stable income and appreciation (potential capital gains). They may be called *income-growth funds* or *growth-income funds.* Still others specialize in preferred stock and some in convertible preferred stock, again with the hope of achieving both income and growth.

There are also *option funds,* whose assets consist of stock options as well as the underlying stocks on which the options are written. These funds were started in 1977 to increase the current income of funds without excessively increasing its risk. The whole concept of options as investments will be made clearer later in this chapter.

Bond funds are mutual funds whose primary objective is safe, steady income, this time in the form of interest. As we saw in Chapter 4, however, bonds also can appreciate, such as when the prevailing interest rate falls, or depreciate, such as when the interest rate rises. *High-grade bond funds* specialize in top-rated bonds with modest yields, but yields that do not fluctuate greatly. *Speculative bond funds* specialize in more risky issues with ratings such as BBB or Baa. Still other funds own mostly low-grade (meaning high-risk) bonds with the uncertain promise of high yields; these are called *junk bond funds*.

There are also bond funds that concentrate on convertible bonds. *Convertible bond funds* earn interest plus a chance for capital gains if the market for common stock (that for which the bond can be converted) rises sharply.

Municipal bond funds are tailored for those investors who want professional management and tax-free income. As described in Chapter 4, tax-free securities generally pay substantially less than equally risky taxable ones. As a result, they are favored mostly by those in higher income tax brackets. Municipal bond funds make tax-free securities available to small investors who are unable to pay $5000 for the typical smallest-denomination municipal bond. However, this still leaves open the question of whether or not small investors should buy tax-free securities at all. Tax-exempt mutual funds were first made available in 1976.

Balanced funds are those which hold varying proportions of stocks, bonds, and preferred stocks. They are most often designed to yield high, steady incomes (income funds) with some appreciation over the long run. These funds are usually conservative and have attracted a rather ho-hum response from investors during the past decade.

There are mutual funds that specialize in the securities of a particular country or group of countries. The oldest and perhaps the best known is the Japan Fund. It allows shareholders to buy into a portfolio of Japanese stocks, something that would be impossible or impractical to do on one's own. Other funds allow investors to buy securities in fast-growing markets, such as that of Norway (up 79 percent in 1983), Hong Kong (up 45 percent in 1984), and Austria (up 172 percent in 1985). Investors wishing to buy Canadian stocks can buy the Calvin Bullock Group Canadian Fund; those wishing Israeli securities can buy the Strategic Israeli Fund. During periods of a depreciating U.S. dollar, *international mutual funds* have outperformed the average U.S. equity fund.

Funds of funds are those which hold neither stocks nor bonds but rather shares in other mutual funds. For investors who cannot decide which mutual fund to buy, funds of funds let them buy (indirectly) a little of several. The disadvantages can be an overdiversification and a compounding of management fees. For example, the overall expense ratio for an investor in Fund Trust (a fund-of-funds mutual fund sponsored by Furman Selz

Mager Dietz and Birney with Republic National Bank of New York serving as its investment advisor) is about 1.75 percent of total assets, compared to the average mutual fund ratio of about 1 percent.

Specialty funds are those which hold assets of firms in a specific industry or firms in industries with a particular distinguishing characteristic. *Gold funds* may hold stock in gold mining companies. *Energy funds* may hold stock in companies producing oil, coal, gas, and/or nuclear power. Other *sector funds* typically invest in one or two industries. Large families of mutual funds, such as Fidelity Investments of Boston or Vanguard Group of Investment Companies, may offer twenty or more sector funds.

Switching among sector funds was a popular investment strategy in the 1930s and 1940s, but it fell out of vogue in the 1950s. In the mid-1980s, the approach was rediscovered, and many investors have become today's "sector rotators." They try to be in energy funds when oil prices are screaming upward, in defense funds when politicians start saber rattling, in health funds when new Medicare benefits are passed by Congress, and so on. If no sector looks especially appealing, most mutual fund groups offer a money market fund where sector rotators can "hide out" until the "bulls" start pushing up a new area.

Of course, the key to successful switching is timing. Sector funds are more volatile than broader mutual funds. Volatility is fine on the way up, but it can be disastrous on the way down. Most financial experts advise against the average investor trying to pick winners and against concentrating large portions of one's portfolio in narrowly defined sectors.

Among specialty funds, there are also those which set moral or ethical parameters for their investments. These *social-conscience funds* may hold securities in firms that deliberately abstain from any activities associated with nuclear energy, the military, or the production of tobacco and alcohol. The Pax World Fund (Portsmouth, N.H., founded by United Methodist Church clergymen in 1971), the Third Century Fund in the Dreyfus group (New York), and the Pioneer Funds (Boston) are "socially responsible" mutual funds. In the mid-1980s, they touted their South Africa–free portfolios, which grew well, although not quite as well as the overall market as measured by the Standard & Poor's 500 Index (*Wall Street Journal,* August 5, 1986, p. 3).

Commodity funds are those holding futures commodity contracts as their principal assets. A *futures contract* is an agreement to deliver (or receive) a certain commodity on a designated date in the future. The contracts are transferable (i.e., salable) and have value until the designated date. Established futures markets in about four dozen commodities ranging from silver to soybeans fluctuate greatly, and the futures contracts themselves are considered highly speculative. Like options, we shall learn more about commodity futures later in this chapter.

CONVENIENCE AND MUTUAL FUNDS

Perhaps the most attractive feature of investing in mutual funds is the convenience that they offer. No other investment provides the diversification at the stroke of a pen that is inherent in the purchase of even one share of a mutual fund. However, mutual funds also provide other services that make investing in them easier, especially for the individual investor with a modest portfolio.

1. *Deposits can be made at any time for any amount* greater than a predetermined nominal figure. A typical fund might require an initial deposit of $300 to open an account but would accept deposits of $50 or more thereafter. Fractional shares eliminate the need to make peculiar investments. If a share of XYZ Mutual Fund costs $12.13 and you wanted to buy $50 worth, you could receive 4.122 shares. There would be no need to buy a whole number of shares, i.e., either 4 or 5, and spend either $48.52 or $60.65. Although a trivial convenience, the ability to invest the exact amount of money you desire can make personal bookkeeping easier for the unsophisticated investor.

2. *Deposits also can be made automatically.* Regular periodic purchases are easily made with mutual funds. As we saw in Chapter 1, such regular periodic investments are essential in the strategy known as *dollar-cost averaging*. And yet small investments are inconvenient and uneconomical (if not impossible) to make in the case of most other financial investments. Consider how you would buy $50 worth of IBM stock each month

or $50 worth of bonds or gold or most any other investment.

3. *Dividends, interest, and capital gains can usually be automatically reinvested* without losing the chance for earnings between the moment they are paid and the time they are reinvested. Unless these earnings are needed for immediate consumption, it is convenient and economical to allow them to accumulate in the form of increased shares or fractional shares. Without automatic reinvestment, the transactions costs in terms of time and planning (if nothing else) of "manually" reinvesting small amounts of earnings exceed the benefits, and instead, the earnings are left idle in a low-yield savings or checking account.

4. *Investments can be easily withdrawn* in several convenient ways. A simple letter (with your signature guaranteed by a bank) is one method. You simply write to the mutual fund and ask to redeem *x* number of shares, or *y* dollars' worth of shares, or the entire amount in your account as of the end of the day on which they receive your letter. Most mutual funds are required to send you a check within 7 days after receiving your letter. (If you are worried about the fund's receiving your letter or acknowledging that they received it, you can send it by certified or registered mail or by special delivery. Ironically, however, both these methods usually take longer than simply sending your request by first-class mail.)

A faster way of withdrawing investments (or "redeeming" your shares) is by wire. You usually set this up at the time you first open your mutual fund account. The fund agrees that upon your written instructions or upon a telephone call from you (where you give your account number and some other identification), they will wire the value of your redeemed shares to your bank account. If you execute a wire transfer before noon, you should have the proceeds available at your bank that same afternoon. This is not only convenient, but it also makes such mutual fund investments far more liquid than stocks, bonds, gold, or almost anything else. For example, you can sell stocks immediately, but you usually have to wait 5 business days before the proceeds are delivered.

A third way of redeeming shares is to have them transferred to a money market fund where you have check-writing privileges. The mechanics of transfer are easy once you have set up an agreement with the mutual fund in which you identify your money market fund and your account number. Like a wire transfer to a bank, you can execute a transfer to a money market fund by either a letter or a phone call—usually on a toll-free number.

5. *Investments can be automatically withdrawn* for those who desire steady income for retirement or whatever other reason. Most mutual funds have a systematic redemption plan whereby you can periodically receive a fixed percentage of your holdings, a fixed dollar amount, a fixed number of shares, or all (or a portion) of just the earnings on your account. Again, such convenience and

flexibility are not offered for most alternative forms of investment.

6. *Investments can be switched from one type of fund to another,* usually with no load charge (even for load funds). Not all mutual funds have switching arrangements with other funds, but most of those in the large families of mutual funds do allow switching. For example, if you are in the Vanguard Group, you can switch, by letter or telephone, from their Morgan Fund to their Windsor Fund to their Money Market Reserve Fund with virtually no transfer costs at all. If you follow the strategy of a switch-hitter (discussed in Chapter 1), such mutual funds are perhaps the single most convenient and economical investment medium—one that avoids having your earnings seriously eroded by transactions costs.

A MUTUAL FUND PROSPECTUS?

A *prospectus* is simply a description of a mutual fund or other financial intermediary. It is a little booklet of information standardized by the Securities and Exchange Commission and required to be presented to prospective investors. (You may write or call for a prospectus and an application; since most mutual funds have a toll-free 800 number, calling is easier.) The main parts of a typical prospectus are

1. *Investment objectives and policies*. This section shows whether the fund is aiming for growth,

income, or both and what kind of investments it is trying to hold in order to achieve these objectives. It also lists restrictions on investments, such as the promise that "the fund will never hold more than 25 percent of its assets in any one industry."

2. *Who manages the fund.* The officers and directors of the fund are listed, along with their connections with other businesses. If the fund employs an advisory service, this is also described.

3. *Who manages the portfolio.* This section tells who does the actual buying and selling for the fund. It also tells who gets the brokerage commissions and the fees for research. There is also a brief description of the custodial bank for the fund. Every fund has a custodian who holds the actual cash and securities.

4. *How to buy shares.* With load funds, this section describes the percentage of the total purchase that goes to the broker or to the salesperson and how the number of shares purchased is determined. No-load funds describe how you can purchase shares by mail, by phone, or through a broker if you insist. Toll-free phone numbers and methods of acceptable payment are also detailed.

5. *Shareholder services.* This section describes special services provided by the fund. These may include the ability to (a) leave shares "on deposit" with the fund (rather than bothering with the physical share certificates), (b) make additional purchases by

phone, by mail, or automatically by preauthorized checks drawn on your checking account and used to automatically buy shares, (c) receive cash or additional shares for the dividends, interest, and capital gains earned, (d) receive written confirmations of each transaction, (e) receive fixed amounts of income periodically (systematic withdrawals), and (f) set up retirement accounts. Other services may include the ability to switch to another mutual fund with no sales charges and with nothing more than a phone call or a letter. Bond funds (and, as we saw in Chapter 2, money market funds) also offer check-writing privileges, so you can write a check that, when cleared, redeems a fractional number of shares whose value is equal to the amount of the check.

6. *How to redeem shares.* This section tells exactly how to redeem shares by phone, by mail, or by some prearranged automatic plan. It also describes redemption fees (rear-end loads), if there are any, and under what conditions these will be imposed.

7. *Accounting and financial statements.* The fund's current balance sheet is listed at the end of the prospectus; it shows all the fund's investments, other assets, and liabilities as of the end of the most recent accounting period. There is also an income statement for the previous fiscal year and a statement showing the changes in the asset values for the past several years. In addition, there may be

a statement about any current litigation against the fund, such as an antitrust suit by the Federal Trade Commission.

A prospectus is a very important source of information for investing in mutual funds. Unfortunately, few investors take the time to even glance through it. Many spend more time reading *Consumer Reports* before buying a particular $500 dishwasher than they do reading the prospectus before buying $50,000 worth of shares in a particular mutual fund.

Depending on the type of assets your mutual fund holds, your investment can range from ultraconservative to very speculative. Our next category of investments can be even more speculative, however. Options are daring investments even when purchased or sold on the most stable blue-chip stocks you can imagine.

OPTION MARKETS
In defending an escaped convict and flimflam man who was accused of fleecing customers out of millions of dollars in options investments, the famous lawyer F. Lee Bailey said, "Options are like crap shooting and nobody who knows anything about investments thinks otherwise" (*Wall Street Journal,* February 14, 1978, p. 1). Although options have existed in one form or another since the seventeenth century, buying and selling them can involve some of the most complicated, speculative, volatile investment decisions you can make.

Part of the complication lies in the jargon used in the

options market. A typical *call option* is the opportunity to buy 100 shares of a particular stock at a certain price within a specified period of time. A *put option* is the opportunity to sell 100 shares of a particular stock at a certain price within a specified period of time. As an investor, you can either buy or sell a call option or buy or sell a put option.

1. If you buy a call option, you buy the right to purchase 100 shares of ABC stock at a fixed price within a certain period of time.
2. If you sell (or write) a call option, you sell someone the right to purchase 100 shares of ABC stock from you at a fixed price within a certain period of time.
3. If you buy a put option, you buy the right to sell 100 shares of (your) ABC stock at a fixed price within a certain period of time.
4. If you sell (or write) a put option, you sell your obligation to buy 100 shares of ABC stock at a fixed price within a certain period of time.

If you think the price of ABC stock will rise, you might like to buy a call option at a price near the current market price. If you are right and the price rises, you can exercise your option and buy the stock at below market value. *Calls are bought with confidence* because their buyers expect the price of the stock to rise.

If you think the price of (your) ABC stock will fall, you can buy a put option that will allow you to sell the stock at a price above the fallen market price. *Puts are bought with pessimism* because their buyers expect the market price will fall. If the market price does not fall, you, the holder of the option, will not exercise it. (Why force a sale on someone when you could sell for more in the open market?) In this case, you will lose only that which you paid to buy the put option, i.e., the premium.

There are four key items in any options contract:

1. The *underlying security*. This is usually a block of 100 shares of a well-known stock such as IBM, Westinghouse, or Alcoa.
2. The *exercise or strike price*. This is the price per share of the underlying security at which the owner of the call option may buy and the owner of the put option may sell. In order to limit the number of options and to make them more standard, strike prices are fixed in multiples of $5 and $10.
3. The *premium*. This is the price paid to the seller or writer of the option by the person who buys the option. It is usually expressed as the premium per share.
4. The *expiration date*. This is the last moment when the option can be exercised. The maximum time span for an option is 9 months. A standard expiration date is the Saturday following the third Friday of the expiration month.

Table 5.1 gives a specific example for put and call options for Avon Products stock. These quotations were

Table 5.1   A Specific Example of Put and Call Options

	Stock	Expiration Date	Strike Price	Premium	Current Price of Underlying Stock
			February 20		
Call	Avon	April	50	1⅝	48⅝
options	Avon	April	60	⅛	48⅝
Put	Avon	April	50	2⅜	48⅝
options	Avon	April	60	12⅛	48⅝

	Stock	Expiration Date	Strike Price	Premium	Current Price of Underlying Stock
			February 27		
Call	Avon	April	50	⅝	45¾
options	Avon	April	60	1/16	45¾
Put	Avon	April	50	4⅛	45¾
options	Avon	April	60	14¼	45¾

reported for February 20 and February 27 for options with expiration dates in April. The price of Avon stock was 48⅝ on February 20 and 45¾ on February 27.

The quotations show that on February 20 you could pay 1⅝ (i.e., $1.625) per share for the opportunity to buy 100 shares of Avon at $50 per share before the expiration date in April. You would only have to pay ⅛ ($0.125) per share for the opportunity to buy 100 shares at $60 per share before the same expiration date. (The premium is lower, reflecting the lower probability that the stock price would be $60 or above by April.)

MAKING A PROFIT ON CALL OPTIONS

If you bought one Avon April 50 call option on February 20, you would have paid $162.50, that is, $1.625 premium per share times 100 shares. At this point, there are two chances for a profit. One chance is that if and when the premium on Avon April 50 options rises above $1\frac{5}{8}$, you could sell the option. Notice, however, that if you sold the option on February 27, when its premium fell to $\frac{5}{8}$, you would have lost $100 on your original $162.50 invested in the option. (Actually, you would have lost even more because of the commissions paid to the broker to buy and then to sell this option.)

The other chance for profit from buying this call option is that the price of Avon stock will rise above $50 at some time before the option expires in April. If it does, you could exercise the option, i.e., buy the stock and immediately resell it, keeping the difference as a gross profit. However, this is not the case, as Table 5.1 shows, if you bought the Avon April 50 on February 20 when Avon stock was $48\frac{5}{8}$ and wanted to exercise and sell it on February 27 when Avon was selling for $45.75. It would be foolish to exercise your (option) right to buy 100 shares of Avon at $50 per share when you could buy it in the open market for $45.75 per share. Again, to exercise and make a profit on this Avon April 50 call option, the price of Avon would have to rise above $50. For example, if the price of Avon rose to $54 per share, your net profit from exercising the option and immediately selling the stock would look like this:

$5400.00	Sale price of 100 shares of Avon at $54 per share
− 5000.00	Purchase price of stock with your option to buy at $50 per share
$ 400.00	Gross profit
− 162.50	Premium paid for the call option
− 150.00	Commissions for the option and to buy and sell the stock
$ 87.50	Net profit

Now go back to Table 5.1 and see what would happen if you had *sold* an April Avon 50 call option instead of buying one. When you sell or write a call option, you give someone the right to buy 100 shares of Avon from you at any time before the option expires. If you sold one Avon April 50 call on February 20, you would have received $162.50 in premiums before commissions. On February 27, you could get out of this agreement by buying back the call option at $62.50 (100 shares times $⅝ per share) plus a broker's commission. Your gross profit would have been $100 per option contract; your net profit would have been lower after commissions.

If you chose not to buy back the call option, and if the price of Avon stayed under 50 until the option agreement expired in April, you would be able to keep the entire $162.50 premium minus commissions and be under no further obligation.

TAKING A LOSS ON CALL OPTIONS

There are three ways to take a loss on a call option. One mentioned above is to buy the option at a higher price than you sell it for, e.g., buy it at 1⅝ on February 20 and sell it for ⅝ on February 27. (Holding it longer might see the price drop further; holding it until the expiration date will surely see the price fall to zero, since an expired option has no value at all.)

A second way to lose is to exercise the option at a sale price above $50 but not far enough above to fully compensate for the option premium and broker's commissions. This strategy minimizes your losses compared to the third case; there you do not exercise the option at all; i.e., you let it expire. In this case, you have nothing to show for the $162.50 premium—it was entirely lost together with the broker's commissions.

When selling a call option on stock you own, you never take a dollar loss. This is known as *writing a covered call.* Suppose you had purchased 300 shares of Avon 3 years ago for $42 per share. On February 20, the stock was 48⅝ per share and you decided to write (sell) three Avon April 50 call options. You would immediately get premiums of $487.50 (three times $162.50 per option agreement) minus a small brokerage commission, say, $30. If the price of Avon falls or stays below $50 per share, the buyer of your call option will not exercise it. You will still have your stock, but as a result of having written the three call options, you are now $457.50 richer ($87.50 minus the $30 commission). If the price of Avon rises above $50, and if your options are exercised, you will get $50 per share for your stock (and, of course, you still keep the net $457.50 in premiums). Selling covered calls is a conservative options investment; you cannot lose in dollar terms. The only thing you can lose is the opportunity to sell your stock at, say, $54 per share instead of the $50 per share if the call is exercised. As a result, many investors write covered calls at prices higher than they paid for the stock on an ongoing basis. If exercised, they make a profit on the stock; if not, they write a new call and collect another premium.

However, if you sell a call option on stock you do not own—a strategy known as "running naked"—you are running a big risk. If you suddenly have to buy the stock at a higher market price than the strike price in order to honor the option you have written, you could have to pay far more than any premium you had received. Using our same example (but not the one shown in Table 5.1), if you wrote five Avon April 50 calls and received $812.50 (five times $162.50 per options agreement) minus a $0 commission, you would be very sorry to see Avon rise to, say, $54 per share and have your options exercised. If this happened, you would have to immediately buy 500 shares of Avon at $54 per share in the market and sell them to the person exercising the options at $50 per share. This would cost you over $2000 with commissions, which is far more than the $772.50 you had received in premiums, net of commissions. Selling (or writing) uncovered options is extremely risky.

MAKING A PROFIT ON PUT OPTIONS

The quotes in Table 5.1 for Avon show that on February 20 you could have bought an Avon April 50 put option for 2⅜ ($2.375) per share or $237.50 for 100 shares. (This option gives you the right to sell your stock at $50 per share.) Only 7 days later you could have sold the same put option for 4⅛ ($4.125) per share. After commissions of $30 to buy and $30 to sell, you would end up with a profit of $115 on your $237.50 investment. This is a 42.9 percent profit for 1 week or an astronomical 1.19 million percent per year! And you did not even have to own the stock. With stakes like these, no wonder Bailey compares options investments to crap shooting:

February 20 bought	one April Avon 50	$ (237.50)
	put commission	(30.00)
February 27 sold	one April Avon 50	412.50
	put commission	(30.00)
Net profit		$ 115.00

Rate of return (for an explanation of this formula, see Chapter 1):

$$(237.50 + 30) (1 + r)^{1/52} = \qquad 412.50 - 30$$

$$(1 + r)^{1/52} = \qquad 1.429$$

$$r = \quad \text{42.9 percent per week,}$$
$$\text{or 1.19 million percent}$$
$$\text{per year}$$

You also could make a profit on buying a put option if the price of Avon stock fell so low that you could exercise the option and sell the stock at $50 per share. These proceeds would have to be large enough to compensate for the premium you paid and for the broker's cost of buying back your stock. In our example, the price fell to $45.75 on February 27. If you exercise your

option to sell your stock at $50, your profit would be
$27.50:

February 20	bought	one April Avon 50	$ (237.50)
		put commission	(30.00)
February 27	bought	100 Avon at $45.75	(4,575.00)
		per share	
		commission	(65.00)
	sold	100 Avon at $50 per	5,000.00
		share under option	
		commission	(65.00)
Net profit			$ 27.50

Unlike buying a put option, selling or writing one can
be profitable if the option is not exercised, i.e., if you are
not forced to buy the stock. In this case, you simply
keep the premium as your profit for having obligated
yourself to buy the stock at a certain price for a limited
period of time. The premium is compensation for the
risk of possibly having to buy stock that has a lower market value.

TAKING A LOSS ON PUT OPTIONS
As mentioned earlier, buying a put option will result in
a loss if the stock does not fall low enough to cause the
price of the put option to increase. The loss will be min-
imized by selling the put before the expiration date. In
the extreme case, you will not exercise the option,
thereby losing the premium you paid and getting nothing

in return. Although the premium paid is your maximum loss, it still represents a 100 percent loss on your options investment.

A more serious loss can occur when you engage in selling a put option on stock when you do not have enough funds to really buy the stock; like selling an uncovered call option, the practice is also known as "running naked." If the buyer forces you to buy the stock and you do not have the funds or must borrow or liquidate other assets to get them, this can be very unprofitable indeed.

ADVANTAGES OF OPTIONS

The principal advantage of investing in options is that they allow you to control more shares of stock than you could if you had to pay for them first in cash. For a relatively small amount (say, $200) in premiums, you can possess the right to buy or sell a large amount (say, $5000) in stocks. The ability to possess assets with less down payment generates leverage. Had you bought $5000 in stocks from a broker, you would have had to put at least $2500 down; with stock purchases, there is a maximum of 50 percent leverage, which is the margin requirement set by the Federal Reserve. However, with stock options, there is 95 to 90 percent leverage in the form of option premiums, which give control (without actual ownership) of the stock for only 5 to 10 percent of the stock's value.

A second advantage is that you need not exercise the option and actually buy and sell stock in order to make a profit. You can buy a call option this month (giving you the right to buy $5000 worth of stock) and sell it to someone else next month for a profit with far less in broker's commissions than would have accrued if you had actually bought and sold the stock itself. The same is true with buying and selling put options, as the Avon example showed.

DISADVANTAGES OF OPTIONS

Options premiums change daily depending on the price of the underlying security and on how much time is left until the option expires. Options with more distant expiration dates usually get higher premiums because there is a greater chance for the price of the underlying security to change.

While leverage can be helpful, it also can lead to greater losses than had the underlying securities themselves been purchased. To the extent that people are attracted by potentially large short-term profits on relatively small outlays, options are closer to horse races, lotteries, and other blatantly speculative investments than they are to traditional investments. (Writing covered call options is the eminently conservative exception.) But fast bucks are usually made in the market only at exceptionally high risk.

Finally, the commissions charged to buy and sell options are decidedly higher than commissions on stock transactions. Full-service brokers often charge 6 to 7 percent of the value of the options, particularly for large numbers of options contracts at low prices and with low total dollar value. Even discount brokers charge 2 to 3 percent for options, although they charge less than 1 percent on stock transactions of similar dollar value.

COMMODITY MARKETS

Unlike *options,* which are rights to buy and sell, *futures contracts* are contracts or obligations to buy or sell. These contracts are on specified amounts of about fifty widely traded commodities, including heating oil, barley, wheat, oats, corn, lumber, sugar, cocoa, pork bellies, copper, gold, and silver. (There are also futures contracts for Treasury bills, notes, and bonds, as well as for foreign exchange, such as German marks, Japanese yen, and Swiss francs.) Historically, these contracts were written by businesspeople who wanted to be sure of paying no more than, say, 10 cents per pound for sugar and by other businesspeople who wanted to be sure that they received no less than, say, $40 per ounce for silver they planned to sell at some date in the future. The desire to shield factor inputs against price fluctuations is still the underlying basis for commodity futures contracts.

However, in a market where some are trying to avoid price fluctuations, others are trying to profit from them. For many people, buying and selling commodity futures has become an extremely speculative (high risk), exciting form of investment—one unhampered by confusing stock reports, prospectuses, and long waits for moderate expected returns. Like some options, commodity futures have become a respectable form of gambling; the numbers printed in the futures price listings of the *Wall*

Street Journal are socially preferred substitutes for the race results printed in the local papers. Some believe that "playing the commodities" and "playing the ponies" are so very similar that to call either an "investment" is to beg the question.

There are currently twelve commodity markets in North America, including the New York Mercantile Exchange, the Chicago Mercantile Exchange, the Chicago Board of Trade, and the Winnipeg Commodity Exchange. These markets look very much like the stock or bond markets except that bids and offers are made here for futures contracts whose terms, other than price, are fixed by each exchange. At the Chicago Mercantile Exchange, the contract for feeder cattle specifies 44,000 pounds of young steers each weighing from 550 to 650 pounds with certain other technical requirements.

Each exchange also dictates the dates on which the futures contracts they trade will expire. This reduces the number of contracts available for buying and selling. For example, feeder cattle contracts expire on precise dates in January, March, April, May, August, September, October, and November. Without such rules, there would conceivably be contracts for every day of the year for different quantities and different qualities of goods—in other words, millions of different futures contracts making chaos out of commodity futures trading.

Many new investors believe that if they buy a contract to purchase 44,000 pounds of feeder cattle at 80 cents per pound next May, they are committed to this agreement and they will have to somehow dispose of the cattle at that time. While this might be true if you were to hold the contract until it expired next May, very few investors are caught in this situation. Instead, sometime before next May you would sell the same contract in the commodity futures market. Of course, you hope you will be able to sell it for more than it was worth when you bought it, but you will most surely sell it anyway—even at a great loss—because the alternative is to end up with about eighty-five feeder cattle worth no more than the value of the contract when it expires. Since virtually no one buys a futures contract who does not later sell it before the expiration date (and since virtually no one sells a contract without later buying it back), brokers base their commissions on "round-trip" orders. (This is an important difference from the options market, where many options are purchased and held until they expire.)

Brokers' commissions are much lower in relation to the total assets bought and sold than they are for stocks, bonds, or other investments. However, because these commissions are generated for short-term in-and-out investments, they rapidly accumulate over the year and can easily add up to 30 percent per year of your assets used to buy and sell commodity futures. Over half the people who buy futures hold them less than 1 week. (On the other hand, options are generally held several months.) At that rate, even a 1 percent broker's commission would amount to 52 percent of the total assets in a continuously invested portfolio committed for 1 year.

Why are futures contracts so speculative? Like options, the primary reason is that as an investor you can exercise great leverage at very low cost. Consider the futures contract to buy 44,000 pounds of feeder cattle at 80 cents per pound. For about $3000 you can buy a futures contract giving you the right (and obligation until you sell it) to own about $35,200 worth of cattle at some specified future date. For $3000 you control $35,200 worth of a commodity, but since you don't actually own the commodity now but only the right and commitment to it in the future, there is no need to pay the balance of the commodity's value. (In the case of buying a stock where you assume immediate ownership, you would have to lay out at least 50 percent—since the margin requirement on stock is currently 50 percent—and you would have to borrow the rest at the going market rate of interest.) Although commodity futures are not priced as a percentage of the value of the underlying goods, they usually cost about 5 to 10 percent of these goods. Thus a commodity futures investor can have 90 to 95 percent leverage compared to a stock investor, who can have at most 50 percent. (The leverage for commodity futures and for options is about the same.)

Higher leverage means higher risk or greater spread of possible returns. Suppose the cattle contract required $3000 down plus a round-trip commission of $100. If the expected value of cattle in May rises from 80 to 85 cents per pound, the value of the contract goes from $35,200 (44,000 pounds times $0.80 per pound) to $37,400 (44,000 times \$0.85 per pound), for a gain of \$2200. If this occurred over the course of 1 year, based on your original outlay of \$3100, you would have a rate of return of 67.7 percent per year:

$$(\text{Down payment} + \text{commission})\,(1 + r)^t = -\text{balance owed on contract} + \text{sale of contract}$$

$$(3000 + 100)(1 + r)^t = -32{,}200 + 37{,}400$$

$$(1 + r)^t = 1.677$$

If $t = 1$ year, then $r = 67.7$ percent per year. However, if the May future price of cattle moved from 80 to 85 cents per pound within 1 month, your annualized rate of return would be 495 percent per year, that is,

$$(1 + r)^{1/12} = 1.677$$

$$1 + r = 496.3$$

$$r = 495.3 \text{ percent per year}$$

And if the May price moved 5 cents per pound in 1 day, which is perfectly possible, your annual rate of return would be astronomical. What other "investment" could you buy for \$3100 and get back \$5200 the same day?

Of course, such leverage causes risk that can result in high losses as well as high gains. Indeed, were it not for the brokers' commissions, the futures market would constitute what economists call a *zero-sum game*. This means that no one person can win unless someone else loses an equal amount; the sum of all the winners' gains is just equal to the sum of all the losers' losses, so the net gain is zero. Since the brokers' commissions are also paid by both the winners and losers, the net gain in the futures market is actually negative.

Remember, futures are contracts. Contracts are made between two parties, even if, as in this case, they do not know each other. If you bought May cattle and made a $2100 profit, someone else sold May cattle and lost $2300. Your broker and the other broker together made $200 for setting up the deal and handling the paperwork.

Let's look at the loser in this case. This "investor" sold May cattle in hopes that the price would fall and he or she could buy back the contract at a lower price. However, luck was not with this person, and as we saw, the price of May cattle rose from 80 to 85 cents per pound. This person's investment looked like this:

$$(\text{Down payment} + \text{commission})(1 + r)^t = \begin{array}{l} \text{proceeds from sale} \\ \text{of contract at} \\ \text{80 cents per pound} \\ - \text{balance owed} \\ \text{on} \\ \text{contract at 85} \\ \text{cents per pound} \end{array}$$

$$(3000 + 100)(1 + r)^t = 35{,}200 - 34{,}400$$

$$(1 + r)^t = \frac{800}{3100}$$

If $t = 1$ year, then $r = -74$ percent per year. In other words, this person put $3100 into this investment and got back $800, resulting in a dollar loss of $2300. Moreover, if the price of May cattle increased further than 87 cents per pound, this person would not only have gotten nothing back, he or she would have had to pay more to close the contract.

INDEX FUTURES

As mentioned previously, commodity futures trading has traditionally been done by businesses seeking to minimize the adverse impacts of changes in prices in the future. (In order to know at what price to sell your Cheerios 9 months from now, it is nice to be sure what you will have to pay for the oats to make them 9 months from now.) However, many individual investors trade futures simply as speculative investments. Since they never plan to take possession of the underlying commodity, there really is no need to have an underlying commodity. All that is really needed is a broadly recognized price or index number on which to base large specified contracts.

In 1982, the Chicago Mercantile Exchange offered its Standard & Poor's 500 futures contract based on the Standard & Poor's broad share-price index. Each index futures contract is equal to the arbitrary weight of 500 times the value of the Standard & Poor's 500 Index at specified future times, such as the last business day in September, December, March, and June. Therefore, if buyers and sellers of these contracts create a market for the March Standard & Poor's 500 Index futures at $275, then each contract is worth 500 times $275, or $137,500. Fluctuations in the current Standard & Poor's Index cause fluctuations in the expected future of Standard & Poor's Index, and the value of a contract can vary greatly.

To play the Standard & Poor's 500 Index "investment" game, you need to put down $10,000 plus the round-trip broker's commission of about $100. Everything else is exactly the same as with any commodity futures investment. Therefore, if you buy March Standard & Poor's 500 Index futures at 275 and the market value of the March Standard & Poor's 500 Index future rises to 280, you can sell them and make a profit of $2500 or $2400 after the round-trip commission:

$$(\text{Down payment} + \text{commission})(1 + r)^t = \quad - \text{ balance of proceeds from buy at 275} + \text{proceeds from sale at 280}$$

$$(10{,}000 + 100)(1 + r)^t = \quad -127{,}500 + 140{,}000$$

$$10{,}100(1 + r)^t = \quad 12{,}500$$

If $t = 1$ year, then $r = 23.8$ percent per year. If $t = 1$ month, then $r = 1191$ percent per year. Again, this is (less than) a zero-sum game. For every winner, there is a loser. In this case, the person who sold the March Standard & Poor's Index futures at 275, hoping they would fall, only to see them rise to 280, took a big loss. His or her investment, which ended in a dollar loss of $2600, would look like this:

$$(\text{Down payment} + \text{commission})(1 + r)^t = \begin{aligned}&-\text{balance of}\\&\text{proceeds from buy}\\&\text{at 280} + \text{proceeds}\\&\text{from sale at 275}\end{aligned}$$

$$(10{,}000 + 100)(1 + r)^t = -130{,}000 + 137{,}500$$

$$10{,}100(1 + r)^t = 7{,}500$$

If $t = 1$ year, then $r = -25.7$ percent per year. If $t = 1$ month, then $r = -97.2$ percent per year.

If you buy an index futures contract hoping to sell it for more if the stock market moves up, it is called a *long hedge* or an *anticipatory hedge*. If you planned to buy stocks, say, 3 months from now, the profits from a long hedge protect you against the higher cost you will have to pay for the stocks in the future.

If you sell an index futures contract hoping to buy it back for less if the stock market moves down, it is called a *short hedge*. If you planned to sell stocks, say, 3 months from now, the profits from a short hedge protect you against the lower proceeds you will get from the stocks you sell in the future.

The Standard & Poor's 500 Index was the first in which index futures were bought and sold. Soon afterward, the Municipal Bond Index, the New York Stock

Exchange Composite Index, the Kansas City Value Line Index, and other indexes also began to be traded.

OPTIONS ON FUTURES CONTRACTS

Not only can you trade commodity and index futures, you also can buy and sell options on most futures contracts. The strike prices are set in fixed increments around the futures commodity price. Therefore, if August cattle are trading around 74 cents per pound, there will be options on these future contracts at 70, 72, 74, 76, 78, and 80 cents per pound. An August 70 call option on August feeder cattle gives the holder the right to buy an August feeder cattle futures contract at 70 cents per pound. If the premium is 2 cents per pound (times 44,000 pounds), it amounts to $880 per option. If August feeder cattle futures rise, the call-option premium will rise; the investor can profit by selling the option or by exercising it to buy the futures contract at less than he or she would have had to pay in the market.

As rights, not obligations, such options are less risky than the underlying futures contracts. Both are highly speculative investments, however. They are suitable only for the most sophisticated investors or for those who clearly recognize them as a form of gambling. As one commentator remarked, "The rich may get richer on such 'investments'; the rest of us should stay away from them."

POINTS TO REMEMBER

¶ A mutual fund is a financial intermediary that sells its own shares to investors and uses the proceeds to buy other assets. This allows the investor to have a piece of a large, diversified portfolio.

¶ Some mutual funds make low-risk investments in high-grade bonds and blue-chip stocks; others purchase very speculative investments that have a high degree of fluctuation in their market values.

¶ Mutual funds provide investment alternatives for small investors. Nominal deposits, automatic reinvestment of gains, and the ease of making purchases and redemptions are common features of mutual funds.

¶ With the exception of writing covered calls, options are more speculative investments, meaning they involve taking greater risks.

¶ A call option is a right to buy at a certain price on or before a certain date.

¶ A put option is the right to sell at a certain price on or before a certain date.

¶ The main reason options have more risk is that they involve a high degree of leverage; i.e., they allow an investor to control a large amount of financial wealth with a relatively small "down payment" or premium.

¶ Commodity futures are futures contracts on specified amounts and qualities of real goods, i.e., commodities.

¶ Commodity futures are highly speculative because they permit potential control of a large amount of valuable goods for a relatively low premium, say, 5 to 10 percent of the value of the underlying commodities.

¶ Index futures and options on index futures are also highly leveraged, speculative investments, and as such, they are not suitable for the average investor.

6

LIFE INSURANCE AS AN INVESTMENT

The primary reason for buying life insurance is to protect against a loss of earnings caused by death. To protect your dependents, you can buy it on your life; to protect yourself, you can buy it on someone else's life, a life in which you have an insurable interest.

A second reason for buying certain kinds of life insurance is for savings (to conserve personal wealth) or for investment (to expand personal wealth). It is this aspect of life insurance that will be the focus of this chapter. However, in order to address the topic of life insurance as an investment, it is important to fully understand the primary function of life insurance, namely, protection, and to separate the pure insurance portion from the savings or investment portion of several different types of insurance policies.

THE OWNER, THE INSURED, AND THE BENEFICIARY

If you buy insurance on your own life, you are both the "owner" and the "insured." As the owner, you can name the "beneficiary," who is the person or institution designated to receive the insurance proceeds in the event of your death. Typically, a person will name his or her spouse and children as beneficiaries.

If you buy insurance on someone else's life, you are the owner and the other person is the insured. In this case, you can either name yourself as the beneficiary or you can name a third party—your children or perhaps some organization such as the Society for the Prevention of Cruelty to Animals (SPCA) or the American Association of Retired Persons (AARP). However, if you buy insurance on someone else's life, you must—by law— have an "insurable interest" in that person's life. Usually you are related by blood or marriage and expect an economic advantage from the insured person's life continuing or an economic loss from that person's death. An insurable interest is also present for a business associate or for a creditor who has an economic interest in seeing that the insured person stays alive.[1]

There are tax advantages to not being both the owner and the insured. In this case, when the insured person dies, the insurance proceeds are not counted in the taxable estate. If the owner dies before the insured person does, only the current value of the insurance policy, not the full face value, is counted in the owner's estate.

In addition to buying insurance for protection or buying it as an investment, there is a third, although less common, reason for buying life insurance, namely, to cover final expenses, such as hospital and funeral expenses. If you want a $20,000 funeral, you have the right to buy insurance to pay for it. You also have the right to insure your own life in order to leave someone else or an institution (charitable, educational, political, or whatever) a legacy. You might have no one who depends or ever will depend on you for economic support, yet if you want to leave a legacy to your college or to your favorite charity, you can do it with life insurance. (Naturally, there are rules to prevent fraud. For example, insurance companies do not usually pay in the case of suicide or in the case of homicide for the purpose of collecting life-insurance money.)

HOW MUCH DO THE "EXPERTS" RECOMMEND? Most "experts" in the field also sell life insurance. Asking such an expert how much life insurance you should have is like asking the president of the Milk Marketing Board how much milk you should drink. With this warning, a general rule of thumb in the industry is that a person with a family to raise should have insurance and other death benefits (Social Security, for example) equal to at least six to seven times his or her current salary. However, for retired people who are less likely to have dependents, the answer to how much life insurance you should have is similar to the answer to how much (whole) milk you should drink—usually very little or none.

As stated earlier, earnings replacement is the largest and most important purpose of life insurance. Remember, the term *earnings* refers to income from labor. It is a portion of total money income; the rest comes in the form of so-called unearned income, i.e., interest, dividends, rents, capital gains, and pension benefits. By definition, retired people are retired from their jobs, meaning they no longer have full-time earnings on which they depend. Their income is largely *unearned,* which is not a derogatory term, but which simply means that it does not come directly from labor. With little in the way of earnings, there is no need for the primary purpose of life insurance—namely, earnings replacement.

Compare two families, one young, the other one retired. With one working spouse, one homemaker, and, say, two dependent children, the young family needs life insurance on the worker's life primarily to replace the earnings of the worker in the event of his or her death. The family also might need insurance on the homemaker's life so that his or her earnings (in the form of real homemaker services) could be replaced in the event of death. Several studies have placed the value of a typical homemaker's services at between $12,000 and $15,000 a year. And this is clearly on the low side for families with several children.

For the retired couple living on Social Security, on investment income, and on pension benefits, the need for life insurance is likely to be far less. If one dies, Social Security and pension benefits may be reduced, but so would be the couple's consumption needs. Investment income is likely to remain unchanged. There may well be other needs or desires for life insurance, but the primary reason—(labor) earnings replacement—does not pertain to most retired people.

In addition to these factors, there are many personal-decision variables that may suggest one's life insurance "should be" different from six to seven times current earnings. The primary consideration is the number of people who are dependent on the insured person's earnings. For single people with no dependents, there is usually little need for any life insurance. The same is true for couples with no children, when both individuals have good jobs or the skills necessary to obtain good jobs. On the other hand, money to pay for dependents' college educations or money to support a mentally handicapped dependent might suggest the need for a higher amount of life insurance.

WHAT DOES THE MARKET OFFER?
Pure, Unadulterated Insurance

There are basically two types of life insurance: "pure" insurance and insurance plus a savings or investment plan. *Term insurance* is a form of pure insurance; it offers protection for a limited period of time, e.g., 5 years. The owner pays a premium each year; if the insured person dies, the beneficiary gets the face value of the insurance policy. If the insured person lives, the beneficiary gets nothing. This is "pure" insurance in the sense that you buy protection and nothing more. There is no savings and no investment. As you get older, the cost of protecting your life increases because your probability of dying within the next year increases and hence you become a greater risk.

Table 6.1 presents the annual premiums for 5-year, constant-value term insurance for selected ages and se-

Table 6.1 First Year Premiums for 5-Year Renewable Term Insurance Issued to Both Men and Women

Age	$50,000	$100,000	$150,000	$200,000	$250,000	$500,000
25	$ 83.25	$111.00	$166.50	$ 222.00	$ 249.75	$ 416.25
30	87.00	116.00	174.00	232.00	261.00	435.00
35	105.00	140.00	210.00	280.00	315.00	525.00
40	145.50	194.00	291.00	388.00	436.50	727.50
45	217.50	290.00	435.00	580.00	652.50	1087.50
50	375.75	501.00	751.50	1002.00	1127.25	1878.75

Source: Teachers Insurance and Annuity Association, 1988.
Note: Since TIAA term insurance is participating, dividends are paid (meaning part of the premium is returned) at the end of each year; the amounts shown above are first-year premiums; after the first year, dividends are used to keep subsequent years' premiums down to a payment equal to the first year's premium.

lected amounts sold by one life insurance company, Teachers Insurance and Annuity Association (TIAA). The data show that there is a first-year annual premium of $111 for a 25-year-old to buy $100,000 worth of protection on his or her life. (Expected dividends are used to keep subsequent premiums at the same $111 level.) It will cost this policyholder the same premium each year for 5 years, after which time the policy will cease. If the owner wishes to renew the policy for the same amount of coverage, he or she will then be 30 years old, and the premium will increase most likely to $116. The data also show that two $100,000 policies cost more than one $200,000 policy, largely because of the increased administrative costs. For all types of life insurance, there are large economies of scale in purchasing larger policies; you get a big "quantity discount."

Insurance Plus Forced Saving

The second basic type of life insurance is a combination of two ingredients—insurance and a savings plan. The most common example of such insurance is a whole-life or straight-life policy. Here the policyholder pays a much larger premium than for similar term insurance. Part of the premium covers the company's cost of insuring the person's life (including administrative costs and insurance company profits), and the other part is "managed" or invested by the company. The latter portion is similar to a forced savings account; it grows as more is added from each successive year's premiums and as interest is compounded over time. Part of the managed portion becomes the *cash surrender value (CSV)* of the policy. If, as the owner, you sell the policy back to the company or cash it in before the insured person dies, you will receive the cash surrender value. (*Note*: You would owe income taxes on the amount by which the cash surrender value exceeds the net premiums paid.) You also may keep the policy, borrow on it up to its loan value (which is about equal to its cash surrender value), and pay interest on this loan.

With whole-life insurance, the cash surrender value increases as annual premiums continue to be paid. If death occurs, however, the beneficiary receives only the face value. Thus the pure insurance portion decreases as the cash surrender value increases, since the pure insurance plus the cash surrender value equals the *face value*. This relationship for a $100,000 policy is represented in Figure 6.1.

Table 6.2 presents premiums for selected ages for $10,000 and $50,000 whole-life policies sold by Savings Bank Life Insurance (SBLI) of New York. The premiums are three to six times more than the premiums for comparable amounts of term insurance. However, unlike the term premiums, which increase every 5 years, the whole-life premiums remain constant. Nevertheless, as shown in Figure 6.1, the amount of pure life insurance that these premiums purchase declines over time.

COMMON TYPES OF LIFE INSURANCE
There are a number of forms of life insurance, the most common of which are listed below. Notice that each one

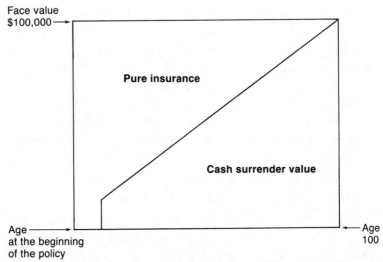

FIGURE 6.1 The pure insurance portion of whole-life insurance declines and the cash surrender value portion increases the longer the policy is kept. There is usually no cash surrender value during the first year or two. Then, the cash surrender value grows until it is equal to the face value at age 100.

represents either pure insurance or insurance plus a savings plan.

1. *Level-term insurance* is pure insurance with a constant value for a set period of time, say, 5 years, for which the premium is fixed. This plan has the lowest premium with constant protection (i.e., a level face value).

2. *Decreasing-term insurance* is pure insurance of declining value written for a set period of time, say, 20 years, for which the premium is fixed. The premiums are

Table 6.2 Annual Premiums for Whole-Life Participating Life Insurance, Male, Nonsmoker

Age	$10,000	$50,000
25	100.20	376.00
30	118.80	469.00
35	144.00	595.00
40	177.30	761.50
45	221.00	980.00
50	279.20	1271.00
55	358.20	1666.00
60	465.80	2204.00
65	616.80	2959.00
70	831.00	4030.00

Source: *Savings Banks Life Insurance Fund, N.Y., N.Y., 1988.*
Note: *The savings bank rates are so low that the insurance industry has exerted political pressure to prohibit out-of-state sales and sales of individual policies greater than $50,000.*

initially lower than comparable level-term insurance, but the premium per dollar of insurance protection rises as the payment at death declines. It is often sold as a "homeowners" or "home-protection" plan to people who want a lot of protection now, when they have a large mortgage, and less protection in the future.

3. *Whole-life insurance* (also called *ordinary life* and *straight life*) is initially pure insurance and gradually becomes more and more of a savings plan. The premium is usually fixed and paid every year throughout the life of the insured person or to age 100.

179

4. *Twenty-payment life insurance* is initially pure insurance, but it moves rapidly over 20 years to become a savings plan. The premium is higher than comparable whole-life coverage; it is fixed and paid only for 20 years. At the end of 20 years, the cash surrender value, which is less than the face value, continues to grow even though premiums are no longer paid.

5. *Paid-up-at-65 life insurance* is the same as 20-payment life insurance except that the premiums are paid for the number of years equal to 65 minus the insured person's present age.

6. *Single-premium life insurance* is paid-up life insurance after one lump-sum payment of $5000 or more. The death benefit exceeds the initial payment, and the cash surrender value grows with tax-deferred earnings. If held until death, there is no tax on the earnings and there is tax-free borrowing up to the amount of the initial lump-sum premium.

7. *Twenty-year endowment insurance* is much more of a savings plan than an insurance plan. Fixed premiums are paid for a 20-year period or until the policyholder dies. If he or she lives 20 years, the policy has a cash surrender value equal to the face value. The premium is higher than that on comparable 20-payment life policies, where the cash surrender value after 20 years is less than the face value.

8. *Age-65 endowment insurance* is the same as a 20-year endowment except that the premium is paid over a number of years equal to 65 minus the age of the policyholder.

9. *Universal-life insurance* is a contemporary form of life insurance that "unbundles" or separates the pure insurance from the savings or investment part of the policy. Because it is quite complicated, we shall first show how to price standard forms of life insurance and then return to a more in-depth look at universal-life insurance.

It should be noted that there are various clauses and riders associated with life insurance policies. A *convertible clause* allows one type of policy to be exchanged for another type. A *guaranteed-insurability rider* allows additional purchases at specified times. A *guaranteed-loan rider* allows the policyholder to borrow at low fixed rates an amount usually equal to the policy's cash surrender value. A *waiver-of-premium rider* is a form of disability insurance that pays the premiums if the policyholder becomes disabled. A *double-indemnity rider* promises double proceeds if the insured person dies in a certain way, e.g., in an accident as opposed to natural causes.

HOW TO COMPARE COSTS FOR LIFE INSURANCE
Life insurance salespeople often claim the net cost to a policyholder (i.e., the owner) is the sum of the premiums paid over a particular period (such as 20 years) minus the sum of dividends the company expects to return to the policyholder, minus any cash surrender value the policy might have at the end of the period. Frequently, this net cost is negative, and the salesperson leads you to believe that if you cashed in the policy after 20 years,

you would have two decades of life insurance and would make a profit as well. You may well scratch your ear, stare at the numbers, and look for that hidden hook.

Here is an example of the net-cost analysis for a $10,000 whole-life policy. Assume the annual premium is $141, the annual expected dividend is $60, and the cash surrender value after 20 years is $2000:

Total premiums for 20 years ($141 × 20)	$2820
Dividends for 20 years ($60 × 20)	− 1200
Net premiums for 20 years	$1620
Cash surrender value after 20 years	− 2000
Net (insurance) cost	$ − 380

Is it possible to buy $10,000 worth of life insurance for 20 years and still get back $380 more than you paid? The answer is "yes" in dollar terms and "no" in real terms.

The following section on the interest-adjusted cost approach is a bit complicated. It is included primarily for those who dislike being asked to accept indexes with no understanding of how they are formulated. This approach is presented to show how the most popular index currently used to compare the costs of traditional forms of life insurance is created and how this index has been developed on exactly the same principles as those used to evaluate any other set of cash inflows and outflows that occur over an extended period of time. The value of careful study and understanding of the interest-adjusted cost approach is not confined to life insurance; it extends to all forms of savings and investment analysis. You do not need to know how the interest-adjusted cost index is formulated to be able to use it, but you do need to know how cash inflows and outflows are reduced or expanded to a common point in time to calculate their aggregate or overall value.

In order to evaluate the cost of our $10,000 whole-life policy, the premiums, dividends, and cash surrender value (*CSV*) must first be adjusted to one point in time. As shown in previous chapters, a dollar received in 20 years is simply not worth the same amount as a dollar received today; the future dollar must be discounted to give its present value or the present dollar must be expanded by the compound interest rate it could have earned if we are to estimate its future or accumulated value.

The rate of 5 percent is commonly used to expand to future value the insurance policy's premiums, dividends, and cash surrender value. This rate is used by insurance companies because they say "it is close to what an individual can expect to earn on a savings account over a long period after making allowances for taxes on the interest earned." However, it is also lower than the market rate of interest today, and it implicitly assumes a zero rate of inflation. Therefore, the 5 percent factor is biased in favor of the insurance companies. With that caveat in mind, all premiums and dividends are first expanded to their future value (*FV*) in, say, 20 years at an annual rate of 5 percent. At the end of 20 years, the policy is assumed to be cashed in. Its cash surrender value (*CSV*) does not have to be expanded because it is already expressed as a future value. Computing the future value of the insurance cost in the preceding example would be done as follows:

Premium: Future value of $141 premium paid at the beginning of each year for 20 years:

$141 × 34.719 = $4895.38

Dividend: Future value of $60 dividend received at the end of each year for 20 years:

$60 × 33.065 = $1983.90

CSV: Future value of $2000 cash surrender value:

$2000.00

Insurance cost for 20 years: Future value of all premiums minus dividends minus the cash surrender value at the end of 20 years:

$4895.38 − $1983.90 − $2000.00 = $911.48

The future value of the insurance cost of the policy evaluated at 5 percent is $911. Now we ask, "How much would one have to put away at the beginning of each year at 5 percent for 20 years to equal this future value of the insurance cost?" Standard statistical tables show

that $1 deposited now at 5 percent and every year here-
after will grow to a future value of $34.719 after 20 years.
Therefore, $911 divided by $34.719 gives us $26.25,
which is the amount paid annually for 20 years that is
equal to a future value of $911. Since it is a $10,000 policy, we can divide by 10 to get an annual equivalent cost
per $1000 of coverage, namely, $2.63 per year per $1000
worth of coverage.

The interest-adjusted cost (IAC) approach gives the
equivalent amount of money the policyholder would
have to pay at the beginning of each year, after accounting for the annual timing of the payments, the dividends,
when he or she might take the cash surrender value, and
the time-discount (or expansion) factor. The IAC approach provides a method of measuring one policy's cost
against another, but it can only be used for the same type
of policy. Five-year term insurance is not the same as
whole-life insurance, and whole-life insurance is not the
same as an endowment policy.

WARNINGS ABOUT THE IAC APPROACH

The IAC approach assumes surrender of the policy. If
the insured person dies, there is no cash surrender value
(*CSV*); there is only the face value of the policy. Therefore, as the cash surrender value increases, the amount
of pure insurance, or the amount that the company is
risking, decreases. (We also saw this in Figure 6.1.)
However, since the premiums remain the same, the real
cost of this insurance is increasing. The IAC approach

does not account for this, except for term insurance, where the issue is avoided because there is no cash surrender value.

The IAC approach also assumes the dividends expected on participating policies will be paid. This is not necessarily the case. If actual dividends are lower than estimated, the IAC may understate the true cost of the policy. Furthermore, the IAC approach assumes that the policies being compared have exactly the same riders for convertibility, renewability, disability, and continued insurability; these attachments vary, however, and their differences are hidden in the IAC approach. So, too, are differences in the growth of the cash surrender value. The IAC approach ranks policies based on cash surrender value at one point in time. The ranking might change if another point in time were selected. For example, based on 20 years, Company A might be cheaper than Company B, but if the cash surrender value of Company B grew more rapidly in the earlier years, a 10-year comparison might have shown Company B to be cheaper than Company A.

Despite these qualifications, the IAC method is far superior to the misleading net-cost method. It gives consumers a more economical way of comparing life insurance. Interest-adjusted costs for policies issued by most life insurance companies are published yearly in *Interest-Adjusted Costs,* a publication of the National Underwriter Company. Perhaps the best explanation and listing of interest-adjusted costs, however, can be found every few years in *Consumer Reports.*

UNIVERSAL-LIFE INSURANCE

By the end of the 1970s, the consumer movement had become so critical of whole-life and other forms of cash-value insurance that the industry began to introduce a new type of policy, one that supposedly separates the pure insurance and the savings portions. Although marketed under different trade names, these new policies became generally known as *universal-life insurance.*

Under the typical universal-life insurance policy, annual premiums are immediately put into a *cash-value account.* From this account a *mortality charge* is withdrawn to pay for the pure insurance or face value of the policy. An *expense charge* is also withdrawn, leaving a reduced net cash value.

How the cash value of a universal-life policy grows depends on the particular company. Some set its "interest rate" each month to reflect the rate of return earned by the company on its investments. Others tie it to the Treasury bill rate or some other well-known index. Still others pay no interest on the first $1000 in cash value, or they may possibly pay higher rates on large cash values, say, those in excess of $100,000. Although most companies have a guaranteed minimum rate (such as 4 percent), the point is that the gross rate of return on the cash value of a universal life policy can vary greatly.

The mortality charge is like the amount paid for pure insurance or simple term insurance. It supposedly reflects the expected death rate of people insured by the company. In fact, though, it can be raised above that at the arbitrary will of the company.

187

The expense charge also can be levied in several different ways. There can be a large front load, such as 30 to 70 percent of the first year's premium, most of which goes to the agent who sold you the policy. In addition, there is usually an annual expense charge (called a *policy* or *administrative fee*) of 5 to 9 percent of each premium. There also might be a back load or expense charge for withdrawals. For example, you might be charged 150 percent of the first year's premium for total withdrawal made during the first 5 years. (These back loads usually decline and are usually not imposed after 10 years.)

The good news about universal-life policies is that they allow flexibility. If you paid a lot in the past so that your current cash value is high enough, you need not make a premium payment this year. Mortality and expense charges will simply be deducted from whatever cash value you now have. Universal-life policies also allow you to increase or decrease the pure insurance coverage under certain guidelines that set minimum and maximum amounts and that may require another medical examination. In addition, like all life insurance cash values, the interest earned (or annual increase in cash value) is tax-deferred and taxable only to the extent that it exceeds the sum of the premiums paid over the life of the policy.

The bad news about universal-life policies is that it is very difficult to recognize one that is a good buy and impossible to predict whether or not it will be a good savings instrument or investment. This problem arises because the value of any particular universal-life policy is a function of three things: the interest rate on its cash value, its mortality charge for pure insurance, and its expense charge. The IAC method described earlier cannot be used to evaluate universal-life policies. Highly advertised rates, such as 12 percent, are no indicator of value because they are likely to be offset by high mortality and expense charges. Moreover, there is no guarantee that these high rates will not be lowered as early as next week. Low mortality charges are also no indicator of value because they, too, can be offset by less interest on cash value and higher expense charges. Furthermore, mortality charges can be drastically raised not just to cover the fact that the insured is getting older, but for the sole purpose of increasing company revenues.

One thing of which you can be sure is that you are likely to get a rate of return that is considerably less than that advertised by companies selling universal-life insurance. If you buy and then cash in a universal-life policy within 5 years, your net rate of return is likely to be negative. For new purchases, most universal-life policies are better buys than whole-life policies, although this definitely does not mean you should trade in an existing whole-life policy to purchase a new universal-life policy. While it is true that the better universal-life policies do not provide a bad rate of return when considered as a savings vehicle, the problem remains how to judge what is a "better" universal-life policy.

SHOPPING FOR LIFE INSURANCE

Salespeople often brag that whole-life and universal-life insurance can be "free" insurance because the owner gets back, in the form of a cash surrender value or cash value, much, all, or more than all of the premiums. However, when premiums, dividends, and cash values are properly adjusted to time, it is clear that there is no such thing as free insurance.

When you purchase an insurance plus savings plan in the form of whole-life insurance, it provides a return on savings only if you, as the insured person, stay alive. If, instead, you cover yourself with low-cost term insurance and put the extra premiums in a savings account, your beneficiaries would receive not only the insurance on your life but the proceeds of the savings account as well. Money put in a simple time-deposit account at 6 percent will double in less than 12 years, and this is a lot better than just getting premiums back in 50 years or more—which is all you accomplish with most whole-life policies. Some universal-life policies allow beneficiaries to get both the face value of the pure insurance portion and the cash-value portion (option B), but their premiums are correspondingly much higher than those which only pay the face value of the pure insurance (option A).

The same salespeople often belittle term insurance as "throwing money down the drain." Such statements are subtle attempts to play on your desire to get something for nothing and to persuade you to buy another type of insurance giving the salesperson a bigger commission. Insurance on a person's life is a good that costs money.

If you do not die, you still did not waste the money in any sense of the word.

Moreover, if you want life insurance, you should buy life insurance, not a combination insurance plus forced savings plan. (The need to be forced to save because you lack self-discipline is another issue.) Term insurance, at low cost for high protection, is the only way most young families can afford the large amount of coverage they may desire. And the fact that the rates rise with age is tempered by the fact that earnings also are expected to rise with age.

When you have decided on the type and amount of life insurance you would like to buy, you should compare the prices of the top twenty companies.[2] It takes a little time, maybe a day or two, but the savings can be thousands of dollars. Consumers Union estimates that a 45-year-old man buying $200,000 of whole-life insurance would be more than $20,000 better off after 20 years if he bought Phoenix Mutual's whole-life policy rather than the identical one sold by Connecticut Mutual under the name Econolife. (*Consumer Reports,* July 1986, p. 400). The Federal Trade Commission bears out this contention. However, even if you save only $2000, where else can you earn $1000 a day for a couple of day's work?

You also should resist advertisements and boasts by the largest or best-known companies, especially since it has been shown that these companies are often not the ones offering the most economical buys. In the 1986 report by Consumers Union, a comparison of $50,000 and $200,000 term and whole-life policies was made covering

136 companies. Among the worst buys (in the judgment of Consumers Union) were policies sold by John Hancock, Metropolitan, Aid Association for Lutherans, and Bankers Life. The point is that best known does not equal best.

Table 6.3 shows the lowest and the highest interest-adjusted costs for 136 well-known companies for a person, age 45, buying a $200,000 policy. The data were gathered by Consumers Union in 1985.

Comparing the interest-adjusted cost indices, whole-life policies look cheaper than term policies, but such a comparison is completely invalid. Whole-life and term policies are two entirely different kinds of insurance, and hence *they cannot, and should not, be compared on the basis of price*. The IAC method may *only* be used to compare the same type of policy issued by different companies.

EVALUATING AN EXISTING
LIFE INSURANCE POLICY

By now it is obvious that the cost of life insurance varies greatly, even among identical kinds of policies sold by well-known companies. The reason for such great disparities is the lack of price competition caused by the lack of understanding on the part of consumers of how to calculate prices. There is, however, a relatively easy way to estimate how much you should be paying for term insurance or for the pure insurance portion of other kinds of life insurance. To do so, find the death rate per 1000 people like yourself. Add a dollar sign and call it

Table 6.3 Range of Interest-Adjusted Costs for a Male, Age 45, Buying $200,000 Worth of Life Insurance*

Type of Policy	Lowest Interest-Adjusted Cost per Year	Highest Interest-Adjusted Cost per Year
5-year renewable term, nonparticipating	$ 556	$1868
5-year renewable term, participating	654	1792
Whole-life, nonparticipating	−1720**	2514
Whole-life, participating	− 520**	662

*For the term insurance, a 10-year IAC 5 percent index was used; for the whole-life, a 20-year IAC 5 percent index was used.
**Negative numbers are not misprints. They reflect the fact that high cash surrender values in the future are discounted by only 5 percent and that these discounted sums more than offset premiums paid minus dividends received.

your expected annual cost per $1000 of pure life insurance coverage. Let's take a specific example and see how this estimate is derived.

Suppose you are a white male aged 65. Table 6.4 shows that the death rate per 1000 white males aged 65 is 24.89. By our rule, you should pay $24.89 for each $1000 worth of life insurance or $2489 for a $100,000 pol-

Table 6.4   Death Rates per 1000 People
and Benchmark Costs of Pure Insurance

| Age | Male | | Female | | Average Death Rate | Benchmark Annual Cost per $1000 Worth of Coverage |
	White	Black	White	Black		
20	1.47	1.89	0.50	0.61	1.01	$ 1.10
25	1.54	2.61	0.50	.94	1.12	1.15
30	1.55	3.61	0.59	1.43	1.23	1.25
35	1.82	4.86	0.80	1.97	1.53	1.50
40	2.46	6.70	1.25	2.91	2.12	2.15
45	3.73	9.14	2.07	4.38	3.25	3.50
50	6.15	13.13	3.46	6.65	5.25	5.50
55	10.35	18.42	5.52	10.30	8.41	8.50
60	16.49	27.16	8.80	15.61	13.12	13.50
65	24.89	36.14	13.45	20.91	19.39	20.00
70	38.54	50.61	20.79	30.37	29.31	30.00
75	58.93	68.24	32.83	42.85	43.96	44.00
80	89.27	95.77	53.59	65.03	67.00	70.00

Source: Statistical Abstract of the United States, 1988, p. 72.

icy. In other words, for every 100,000 white males aged 65, the data show that 2489 are likely to die this coming year. If an insurance company sold $100,000 policies to 100,000 white males aged 65 and charged $2489 for each policy, they could expect to collect $248,900,000 in premiums and pay out $248,900,000 in insurance benefits, or $100,000 for each of the 2489 people expected to die. In other words, charging $2489 for $100,000 policies covering men in this age group would lead the company to expect payouts to be equal to premiums collected.

At this point, you may well ask, "How could a company that charged premiums per $1000 worth of coverage that are exactly equal to death rates per 1000 people ever make a profit?" The answer is that the mortality rates shown in these data overstate the mortality rates for many preferred groups for whom the insurance company agrees to write policies. For example, the Teachers Insurance and Annuity Association (TIAA) insures men and women, white and black, whose average death rate is about one-third less than that shown in Table 6.4 for white males. Insurance companies do not insure everyone. Disease, chronic illness, high blood pressure, drug addiction, dangerous employment, and other such factors can cause a person to be uninsurable. The people that companies do accept have much lower mortality rates than the population as a whole. College teachers, especially those with tenure, are particularly "insurable," because they are more likely to maintain their health (eat regularly, reduce sugar and salt consumption, abstain from smoking, exercise frequently) and because their employment is neither dangerous nor particularly stressful. And even for people they do insure, companies do not always pay benefits when the insured dies. Death caused by suicide, hang gliding, parachute jumping, and as a result of injuries associated with a particularly dangerous occupation is often exempted from benefits.

A second reason the death rates shown in Table 6.4 overstate the cost of pure insurance is that there is a time factor between the point when the premiums are paid by the owner of the policy and the point when the death benefits are paid by the company. During this time, the insurance company is earning interest on the premiums it has collected. In this day and age, the interest earned on premiums held by life insurance companies, even in their most conservative investments, is 7 to 10 percent per year.

There is a strong temptation to conclude that if your life insurance costs more per $1000 worth of coverage than your death rate per 1000 people, you are being overcharged. However, while this may be true from an actuarial standpoint, notice the great differences among death rates. Black males aged 65 have a death rate that is about 45 percent higher than their white counterparts. Should they be charged 45 percent more? White females aged 65 have a death rate that is 46 percent lower than their male counterparts. Should they be charged 46 percent less? Further categorization by occupation and by certain health habits (such as smoking versus nonsmoking) would lead to even greater differences in death rates even for people who are the same age, sex, and race. Consequently, a benchmark annual cost per $1000 coverage that is slightly higher than the overall death rate can be established, as shown in Table 6.4.

Against these benchmark costs (per $1000 worth of coverage), the annual costs of particular policies can be compared. However, first you must calculate the annual cost per $1000 of the pure insurance portion in your existing policy. To make this calculation you will need to know the following:

$P:$ The annual premium at the beginning of the policy year

$CVP:$ The cash surrender value at the beginning of the policy year

$CV:$ The cash surrender value at the end of the policy year

$D:$ The annual dividend paid at the end of the policy year

$F:$ The face value of the policy

You also will need to "time adjust" values at the beginning of the period to get their future or "accumulated value" at the end of the year. We shall set this interest-adjustment factor i at 5 percent. Putting this information into the following formula gives you the annual cost per $1000 worth of coverage for this year:

$$\frac{(P + CVP)(1 + i) - (CV + D)}{(F - CV)/1000}$$

= this year's cost of the pure insurance
per $1000 worth of coverage

The top portion of the formula says, take your premium plus the cash surrender value at the beginning of the year, adjust it for time to its equivalent value at the end of the year, and subtract what it is worth at the end of the year (namely, its new cash surrender value plus any dividend you might get). Divide this by the amount of pure insurance (which is the face value minus what you could have surrendered the policy for at the end of the year), divided by 1000 to get the latest annual cost per $1000 worth of coverage.

For nonparticipating term insurance, the computation is easy because there are no dividends and there is no cash surrender value. A typical $200,000 nonparticipating term insurance policy with an annual premium of $500 for a 45-year-old would have an annual cost per $1000 coverage of

$$\frac{\$500(1.05)}{\$200,000/1000} = \$2.63 \text{ for each } \$1000 \text{ worth of coverage}$$

Notice that this cost is well below our benchmark of $3.50 per $1000 coverage for a person this age. The most expensive $200,000 nonparticipating term policy surveyed by *Consumer Reports* had a cost of $6.72 per $1000 per year of pure insurance coverage, not quite double our benchmark. Even this is not bad, however, when compared to the cost of pure insurance for a typical comparable whole-life policy. For such a policy, we are likely to see

$$P = \$\ \ 4,500$$

$$CVP = \ \ 10,000$$

$$CV = \ \ 10,500$$

$$D = \ \ \ \ 500$$

$$F = \$200,000$$

Using our formula, we get

$$\frac{(4500\ +\ 10,000)\ (1.05)\ -\ (10,500\ +\ 500)}{(200,000\ -\ 10,500)/1000}$$

= $22.29 for each $1000 of pure insurance coverage

The cost of this whole-life insurance coverage is more than six times our benchmark cost of $3.50 per $1000 worth of coverage. It is little wonder that most consumer advocates recommend "buy term; invest the difference elsewhere." (The best discussion of the creation and use of benchmark costs can be found in the *Insurance Forum,* Vol 9., No. 6, June 1982. Its editor, Professor Joseph Belth, is one of the most knowledgeable consumerists in the insurance field.)

"BUY TERM; INVEST THE DIFFERENCE ELSEWHERE"

Most financial counselors advise families first to secure the life insurance protection they need and then to accumulate savings or invest in a variety of ways, which only rarely include buying high-premium life insurance policies. This advice is almost unanimously followed by college and university employees, over 90 percent of whom choose level-premium term insurance offered by the Teachers Insurance and Annuity Association (TIAA). (About 50 percent of the total population now purchases term insurance.) It is unlikely that the debate over whether term, whole-life, universal-life, or some other cash-value insurance is "better" will ever be resolved. The two forms of life insurance are inherently different and hence are not subject to exact comparison as to which is better. Nevertheless, consumer advocates and personal finance experts overwhelmingly recommend term policies and generally steer people away from the many varieties of insurance plus saving policies that are so strongly pushed by those in the insurance industry.

The answer to the question, "When is a buy-term-invest-the-difference strategy preferable to a buy-cash-value-let-the-company-save-part-of-your-premiums-for-you-strategy?" lies in a comparison of the net rate paid on the savings portion by the insurance company with the comparable rate you could earn on relatively safe investments. These savings portion rates of return are difficult to calculate and are well hidden from the consumer. However, they have been very low historically. In a 1973 congressional study, most policies were found to pay rates of return on their savings elements of only 0.5 to 3.5 percent, although a few paid as much as 5.2 percent (*1976·Interest-Adjusted Index.* Cincinnati: National Underwriter Company, 1976, p. xxvi). In 1974, "the Society of Actuaries reported that 38 percent of the 144 best selling (whole-life policies) had *negative* average rates of return after 10 years. After 20 years, the average return was 3½ percent, with 5 percent tops" (*Business Week,* February 5, 1979, p. 85). Even some of the newer universal-life policies' cash values yielded net rates of return after 5 years as low as *minus* 10.15 percent per year and after 20 years as low as 6.26 percent per year. A 1977 Federal Trade Commission study confirmed these findings; it claimed that the typical whole-life policy yielded an average return on the savings portion of only 1.3 percent (A. O. Sulzberger, "Report on Whole-Life Insurance Says Buyers Lose Billions Yearly," *New York Times,* July 11, 1979, p. A14). Since passbook savings accounts pay at least 5 percent, most people would be better off to buy term insurance and put the premiums saved (the difference between those they would have paid had they bought cash-value insurance) in a simple savings account. This is true even after considering that interest earned on a savings account is not tax-deferred.

An equally serious problem is that many policyholders simply forego any chance of reaping the benefits of the savings portion of their life insurance. Twenty percent of all policies purchased are terminated or converted to term insurance within the first year, resulting in lost savings in excess of $200 million annually. In the words of an actuarial expert with the New Jersey Department of Insurance, "each sale of (whole-life) insurance should be preceded by a caution, in bold red letters, saying: 'Warning: The Insurer General has determined that this policy is going to cost you a hell of a lot of money if you don't intend to keep it in force for more than a year or two.'"

SHOULD YOU BORROW ON
A LIFE INSURANCE POLICY?

One of the attractions of buying most insurance plus savings policies is that you can borrow on them up to the maximum loan value. This loan value increases each year and is about equal to or slightly higher than the cash surrender value. The interest you must pay is specified in the policy; it is typically between 6 and 9 percent.

This automatic loan feature is attractive to those who would otherwise be making personal loans at higher rates. It is also attractive to those people who can earn more interest than that charged on the insurance loan. If you borrow $10,000 on your life insurance policy at 6 percent and invest it in, say, a certificate of deposit (CD) at 10 percent, you will generate $400 in net interest (before taxes) each year. This may not sound like much, but all you had to do was apply for the loan with your insurance company and use the proceeds to buy the CD.

The insurance company will try to get you to pay back the loan. They will tell you that failure to do so will mean an equal reduction in death benefits to your beneficiaries. This is no problem, however, since you already have the money, and it will go into your estate, where your survivors will get it anyway.

As long as you can earn a higher rate of interest than that charged on your life insurance loan, it is always profitable to borrow the full loan value and invest it. As long as your investment (in this case the CD) returns higher yields, there is no financial incentive to pay back the life insurance loan.

POINTS TO REMEMBER

¶ Because your demand for life insurance depends primarily on your desire to meet your survivors' financial needs, you should first define these needs and then see to what extent they would already be met from your personal wealth, from Social Security, and from other existing death benefits. Since this calculation can be quite difficult, insurance experts recommend holding insurance six to seven times your current earnings.

¶ Term insurance is pure life insurance; whole-life insurance and policies with cash values combine life insurance with a forced saving plan.

¶ You can purchase far more insurance coverage per premium dollar with term insurance than with any other kind.

¶ Universal-life insurance separates life insurance into a distinct portion for pure insurance and one for cash value.

¶ The value of universal-life insurance depends on three things: the interest rate on the cash-value portion, the mortality charge, and the expense charge. Since there is no way to combine these into a single index and no way to predict what they will be in the future, comparisons among universal-life policies are difficult or impossible to make.

¶ The interest-adjusted cost (IAC) approach is a method of reducing a series of payments (premiums) and receipts (dividends and cash surrender value) to a single number.

¶ While the IAC approach is the most widely recognized method of comparing the same type of traditional policies offered by several different companies, it cannot be used to compare universal-life insurance policies.

¶ When shopping for life insurance, remember there is no such thing as free insurance; if there is no direct charge, there will certainly be an indirect one.

¶ Remember also that insurance payments are never "wasted" just because the insured person does not die during the life of the policy; the protection afforded by the insurance is what you are really paying for.

¶ The lowest cost per $1000 worth of pure insurance should be about the same as the death rate per 1000 people like the insured. From these rates, benchmark costs per $1000 worth of coverage are established against which the annual cost per $1000 coverage for an existing policy can be compared.

¶ While there are exceptions, most personal financial planners (who do not sell life insurance) agree that pure life insurance serves a very necessary function, namely, protection for dependents against loss of earnings of the insured due to death.

¶ However, as an investment, life insurance has a poor track record. Cash-value policies are difficult to assess, unreliable in the future, and not likely to yield net rates of return equal to other comparably risky financial investments.

¶ As long as you can earn a higher rate of interest than that charged on your life insurance loan, it is always profitable to borrow the full loan value and invest it.

7

REAL ESTATE AS AN INVESTMENT

Most owner-occupied housing is held primarily for its housing services. While it may have investment aspects, its primary function is the consumption of its services of shelter, convenience, and social status. On the other hand, when real estate is held strictly with the expectation of getting a stream of returns and/or an appreciation in market value, it can be treated as an investment. Real estate held for investment can be either owned or leased. (Leased real estate can provide a stream of returns but usually not a capital gain.) The important thing is that the investment is expected to generate a stream of returns, an appreciation in value, or both.

Some real estate is valued as an investment primarily for its stream of expected returns. An office building, a store, or a parking lot falls into this category. The expected returns can be monetary (such as rents and parking fees), or they can be real returns with monetary value. There may be an expected appreciation in the market value of these properties, or there may be an expected depreciation. For example, a building might be expected to appreciate or depreciate in value; on the other hand, mineral rights will more likely depreciate as the minerals are extracted.

Other real estate is valued as an investment not for its expected returns, but primarily for its expected appreciation. Vacant land is one example. Here the expected returns are actually negative, since taxes, interest, maintenance (e.g., mowing the grass), and insurance costs continue even though no income is produced. Unharvested (growing) stands of timber and unmined mineral rights are other examples. Such real estate investments are purely speculative in nature and are very similar to other tangible investments such as gold, silver, diamonds, and collectibles.

Real estate deserves special attention as an investment because, overall, its appreciation has been the single most important source of personal wealth for middle-income individuals and families. This does not mean, however, that it is the ideal investment and that your particular property will increase in value. It is unwise to reason that just because "they're not making any more land," your parcel is destined to rise in value.

Real estate also deserves attention because it is usually held for longer periods of time, during which there may be many expected and unexpected receipts and expenditures (positive and negative returns). The timing and the nature of these returns, and particularly the tax consequences associated with them, make calculating the yield on real estate investments difficult. Moreover, even if yields are estimated, it is often not easy to compare them with the yields on other kinds of investments, such as stocks and bonds. Real estate is more illiquid, more leveraged, and more affected by tax considerations than are most alternative investments.

ADVANTAGES OF REAL ESTATE INVESTMENTS
Although the yield on any investment is a function of its stream of returns and its appreciation, these are not the only attractions of investments in real estate. There are many other positive aspects, such as the degree of leverage, the compulsion to save, the desirability of owning something tangible, and the tax treatment of the expected returns and appreciation. Taken individually, these advantages are not always unique to real estate. Nevertheless, investments in real estate do provide a unique combination of these advantages.

Leverage
As we have seen in previous chapters, *leverage* is defined as the ratio of debt to equity for a particular asset or group of assets. Leverage can be desirable if it increases the possible rates of return on an investment.

Most real estate can be purchased with a 5 to 30 percent down payment and a 95 to 70 percent mortgage. This means that most real estate can be purchased with initial leverage of 95 to 70 percent. On a $100,000 piece of property purchased with an $80,000 mortgage, the leverage would be

$$\frac{\text{Debt}}{\text{Equity}} = \frac{\$80,000}{\$100,000} = 80 \text{ percent}$$

(*Note:* The word *equity* is sometimes used to describe how much you would have if you liquidated the property and paid off any debts on it. In this sense, your equity would only be $20,000. But *equity,* as it is used here, describes the full value of the asset that you own, i.e., that you have title to and control over.)

Real estate investments allow people who would otherwise have difficulty in borrowing large sums of money to get into debt and enjoy the possible financial rewards (and losses) associated with more highly leveraged assets. With $20,000 down, no bank will allow you to borrow $80,000 to buy $100,000 worth of stocks or mutual funds. However, the same bank might readily grant you an $80,000 mortgage to buy a $100,000 two-family home. As such, real estate is one type of investment that generally lets you increase your leverage.

Forced Savings

A second advantage of real estate investments is that they often tie you into a compulsory savings plan. Once you have gotten a mortgage to buy real estate, you are (usually) bound to pay regular installments to amortize this debt. The portion of these installments you are "forced" to pay toward the principal (as opposed to the portion you pay for interest) is a form of compulsory savings. To this extent, investments in real estate are similar to investments in whole-life or universal-life insurance, where a portion of the premium you pay goes toward the cash value. Naturally, you are not legally forced to save, but failure to continue with the mortgage payments (or life insurance premiums) inevitably will mean having to liquidate or give up the asset. In other words, failure to save results in foreclosure of the mortgage or cancellation of the policy.

Owning Something Tangible

The third advantage of any investment in real estate is more romantic than economic in nature. It is the advantage of being able to see your investment, to touch it, to "dig" it (or literally to dig in it if you prefer). With a real estate investment, you can walk its boundaries. On it you can build a house, grow potatoes, have a party, camp out, or do any number of other things—all subject to the laws of nature and the laws set down by the local zoning authority. You can do none of these things on a stock certificate. Perhaps these are all foolish reasons from the standpoint of cold, hard, personal financial decision making, but there are a great many people who invest in real estate for exactly these tangible qualities.

TAX ADVANTAGES FOR REAL ESTATE INVESTMENTS

It is one thing to expect a stream of returns or appreciation from an investment. It is another to keep part of these yields for yourself or to protect them from the ever-present tax authorities. Investments in real estate—

and especially the investment portion of your principal residence—are blessed with many tax advantages, some of which are only granted to this kind of investment. Consider these four tax advantages: (1) deductions for interest and property taxes, (2) deductions for depreciation, (3) deferral of capital gains, and (4) exclusion of capital gains.

Deductions for Interest and Property Taxes

Many people invest in real estate with the illusion that among its main advantages are the tax write-offs for interest paid on the mortgage and for property taxes. Some are so naive as to think that interest and property taxes cost investors in real estate nothing because "these expenses are just taken off the income taxes they would otherwise have to pay." Even if you itemize, these expenses are only deductions; they are not credits that reduce your taxes dollar for dollar.

Interest paid on a mortgage is the cost to you of having borrowed money. On your principal residence, mortgage interest can be used as a deduction to reduce taxable income, but only if itemized deductions are already above a certain level that depends on your filing status. If your other itemized deductions are low, the impact of deducting mortgage interest could be very small or nonexistent. The same is true for property tax payments. However, even if other itemized deductions are high, interest and property tax expenses reduce income taxes only up to your marginal tax bracket. For example, if your marginal tax bracket is 28 percent, $3000 in mortgage interest and property tax payments would reduce your income tax burden by only $840 at best.

Despite these sobering facts, deduction allowances for interest and property taxes do mean that these expenses can cost you less than their face value after their impact on taxes is considered. The deductibility of interest and property tax expenses are advantages, although the expenses themselves represent negative expected returns.

Deductions for Depreciation

People who specialize in real estate investments recognize the unique tax advantage of orchestrating book depreciation for their investments regardless of the fact that the actual market value of their assets might be rising. The idea is to "write off" the largest portion of the value of the buildings and other structures that depreciate, not necessarily in a physical sense, but rather in an accounting sense. The depreciation write-offs allowed under the tax laws can mean large savings on current income taxes. More important, there need be no actual costs or negative returns in order to create the deduction. For all practical purposes, this deduction can be created without regard to actual changes in the investment's value.

Suppose you and I each own a $250,000 apartment building and are allowed to depreciate it at the rate of $10,000 each year for the next 25 years. If we are both in the 35 percent marginal tax bracket, the depreciation allowance will be worth $3500 in tax savings to each of us each year. At the end of that time, our properties will have, for tax purposes, the capital value of zero.

Now suppose that after 25 years you sell me your property and I sell you mine and that the sale price of each is $250,000. Both of us will then owe a tax on a capital gain equal to the sale price. Prior to 1987, the taxable portion of that capital gain was only $100,000, since there was a 60 percent exclusion on long-term capital gains. In the 35 percent tax bracket, this gain meant an actual tax of $35,000. However, even with no capital gains exclusion, the present value of the 25 years of tax benefits due to depreciation is greater than the present value of the current capital gains tax. Now with our "new" properties (I with yours and you with mine) we can begin all over again to depreciate them for tax purposes.

Neglecting all transfer costs, appreciation, and other complications, we each saved $87,500 ($3500 per year times 25 years) in taxes during the 25 years and paid $87,500 in capital gains taxes in the last year. However, the present value of the $3500 saved each year for the past 25 years, evaluated at 8 percent, is $255,870. Compared with the current taxes of $87,500 ($250,000 $\times$ 0.35), the difference, $168,370, represents the present value of the tax savings (measured at the end of the investment). This value is equivalent to $24,585 twenty-five years ago, that is, $168,370 $/1.08^{25}$. If capital gains exclusions are reintroduced, as they are likely to be, these tax savings due to depreciation would be even greater.

Depreciation allowances are restricted to real estate investments and to real capital investments, such as machinery. It is not possible to depreciate vacant land. Nor is it possible to depreciate your own residence, although you may depreciate a portion of it if it is used for business purposes (such as an office at home). Depreciation cannot be taken on financial investments, such as stocks and bonds, nor can it be taken on tangible investments, such as gold and diamonds. However, for certain real estate investments, depreciation is an ideal tax loophole.

Deferral of Certain Capital Gains

Another big tax advantage is related specifically to any capital gain made on real estate used as your principal residence. The tax benefit is that the capital gain need not be taxed for the year when the property is sold. In fact, the gain can be deferred indefinitely, and as we shall see below, it might someday be excluded altogether. The main criterion that allows capital gains deferral is that within 2 years you buy or build a new principal residence at least equal to the amount received from the sale of the old one.

A capital gain made on residence 1 is subtracted from the purchase price of residence 2. Other additions and subtractions are also made to arrive at the adjusted purchase price and adjusted sale price for each residence. For example, if residence 1 had an adjusted purchase price of $20,000 and an adjusted sale price of $130,000, your capital gain would be $110,000. If residence 2 has a purchase price of $132,000, it would be lowered to an adjusted purchase price of $22,000 to reflect the deferred capital gain of $110,000. Now if residence 2 were sold for $140,000, there would be a capital gain of $118,000. If residence 3 were purchased for $155,000, its adjusted purchase price would be $37,000 to reflect the two previous capital gains, whose sum is $118,000. Then if residence 3 were sold for $175,000, there would be $138,000 in total capital gains accrued over the purchase and sale of all three houses.

If no new residence is purchased or built within 2 years, that $138,000 capital gain would be taxed. If you were in the 28 percent marginal tax bracket and if capital gains continue to be taxed as ordinary income, the (extra) tax on this gain would be $38,640 (i.e., $138,000 in capital gains times 28 percent). However, this tax could still be deferred if residence 4 costing $190,000 were bought. Its adjusted purchase price for future capital gains computations would be $52,000.

(*Note:* With generally rising prices, most people who buy real estate experience appreciation in their property value and hence a capital gain when they sell it. Nevertheless, there are many properties that for one reason or another depreciate in market value. The IRS does not allow a loss on a personal residence to be deducted, nor does it even allow the owner to increase the cost basis of the next house he or she purchases.)

As this buying and selling continues through the years, the taxes on the capital gains are continually deferred. (There are two other conditions necessary for continued deferral of capital gains taxes. First, not more than one principal residence may be bought and sold within a 2-year period, and second, a new residence cannot be purchased and resold before an older home is resold.) The IRS has made these capital gains even more desirable by excluding (subject to certain conditions) the first $125,000 of them from any taxes whatsoever.

Exclusion of Certain Capital Gains

If you qualify, the IRS may allow you to exclude up to $125,000 of long-term capital gains made on the sale of certain real estate. In order to do so, these conditions must be met:

¶ You or your spouse (if the property is jointly owned) must be age 55 or over.
¶ The property must have been your principal residence.
¶ You can take the exclusion only once, and you cannot take it if your spouse ever used it, even in a former marriage.
¶ You cannot have used part of the exclusion previously. This means it is a one-time exclusion and it is not cumulative. If you have a gain of only $30,000 and choose to exclude it now, you cannot ever exclude any similar future gains; the other $95,000 exclusion is forfeited forever.

The *capital gain* is computed by taking the adjusted sale price and subtracting the adjusted purchase price. The *adjusted sale price* equals the sale price of the property minus broker commissions, other sale costs, and fix-up expenses made within 90 days of the sale. The *adjusted purchase price* equals the purchase price plus transfer costs (lawyer's fees, mortgage fees, title insurance, appraisal fees, etc.) and capital improvements minus capital gains deferred from previously owned home(s). The adjusted sale price minus the adjusted purchase price equals the capital gain.

This $125,000 capital gains exclusion can be a very valuable aspect in your financial planning for retirement. At age 55, you could be earning more than ever before; if so, your marginal tax bracket might be very high. If a large capital gain were to be added on top of your other current income, your taxes would increase significantly. Suppose you have a capital gain of $200,000 and you are currently in the 40 percent (federal, state, and local) tax bracket. If you are in the 40 percent tax bracket, this could mean extra taxes of $80,000. However, if you are able to exclude the first $125,000 in capital gains from the sale of a principal residence, you could save $50,000 in taxes for which you would otherwise have been liable. With the exclusion, your $200,000 capital gain would cost you "only" $30,000 in income taxes, even though you are in the 40 percent tax bracket.

Given the potential benefit from this large exclusion, it is important to plan and qualify for it. For example, delaying the sale of a principal residence to age 55 or later could mean a large tax benefit that would not have been possible at age 54 or younger. On the other hand, once you qualify to exclude part or all of such a capital gain, your decision as to whether or not to purchase other housing will affect your decision on whether or not to exercise the capital gains exclusion. For example, why use your exclusion now to avoid paying taxes on a $30,000 gain when you could delay capital gains taxes by buying more expensive housing on which you might increase your future capital gains and your future exclusion? Remember, to exclude the $30,000 gain today prevents you from excluding even bigger gains tomorrow.

Finally, it is important to emphasize that this exclusion applies only to your principal residence. It is a big factor in the investment value of such property, but it is irrelevant for the value of other real estate, such as an apartment house, held strictly for investment purposes. There is no exclusion for capital gains made for any other type of real estate—residential, commercial, or industrial; it is allowed only for gains made on your principal residence. Nevertheless, it is a unique advantage for this type of real estate investment and an advantage not applicable to the capital gains made on any other type of investment, either real or financial.

DISADVANTAGES OF REAL ESTATE INVESTMENTS

So far we have seen that the positive aspects associated with an investment in real estate make it quite different from alternative investments in financial securities. Before plunging into real estate investments, however, we should note that they are also distinguished by several decidedly negative aspects. These include visibility, accountability, illiquidity, the danger of overinvestment, and the burden of relatively high transactions costs.

Visibility

Ownership of real estate almost always subjects you to its visibility. Your name is on the deed, the title transfer is announced in the local newspaper, and your owner-ship is officially a matter of public record. Anybody can find out how much property you own in a particular county by simply looking up your name in the recorder's office at the county court house. Long before an inves-tigator (tax agent, private eye for your estranged spouse, researcher, or curiosity seeker) could find out how much you hold in stocks, bonds, other securities, cash, per-sonal property, annuities, and life insurance equity, he or she could find how much real estate you own, at least in the immediate area. It is the one asset that is the easiest to find or, from another point of view, the most difficult to hide.

So what is so bad about real estate's visibility? Noth-ing as long as you do not mind or are not sensitive to others knowing and judging you by your wealth hold-ings. However, many people are sensitive about this and choose to hold lower-profile or less-conspicuous forms of wealth. Holding less-visible assets may reduce pres-sure to contribute when you do not really want to do so. Your actions are less likely to be the topic of local gossip, and you and your family can lead more private lives. Moreover, both you and your children are not as likely to be prejudged—often misjudged—as being "rich" in a derogatory sense. When one kid accusingly says to another, "You're rich; your father owns Sunset Manor Apartments and charges rip-off rents," the perception might be totally false. The apartment complex might in fact be heavily mortgaged or even in the red, yet the face value of the entire property is taken as a proxy for the parent's personal wealth.

It also might be tiring, if not embarrassing, to try to explain that your purchase of a duplex (a two-apartment building) for $60,000 and your sale of the same property 2 years later for $150,000 was actually a loss and not the investment coup that everyone seems to think it was. Acquaintances fail to see the $4000 you paid in purchasing closing costs, the $12,000 in interest, the $10,000 for a new furnace, the $6000 for a new roof, the $14,000 for utilities, the $2000 for insurance, the $30,000 for interior remodeling, the $5000 for property taxes, the $10,000 for selling costs (mostly broker's fees), and the capital gains taxes, all of which created a net loss on this real estate venture. All they can see is that you bought a place, held it for 2 years, had "big tax write-offs," and made a "fat" $90,000 ($150,000 minus $60,000) more than you originally paid. None of this might have come up if your investment had been less visible.

Accountability

Ownership of real estate also leads to a greater degree of accountability than does ownership of most alternative investments. If you own the duplex mentioned above, you would be accountable to your tenants for proper maintenance and other conditions specified or implied in their leases. If you own a miniature golf course, you would be responsible for maintenance, lighting, and safety associated with that particular business. (Of course, you could lease the business to some other party, but even then you, as the owner, are still accountable, at least to some degree.) Even if you own a vacant lot, you may be liable for injuries suffered by another person who trespasses on your property. Such accountability and liability are certainly not costs associated with ownership of stocks, bonds, and other securities.

Illiquidity

As was mentioned in previous chapters, ownership of real estate also implies the negative aspect of *illiquidity*. Land and buildings are not generally assets that can be dumped on the market and liquidated on short notice. While you can sell a million dollar block of stock within hours, it may take months to get the fair market price for a million dollar piece of land. The reason is that the market for real estate is much "thinner," meaning that there are fewer willing buyers and sellers at any given point in time. Moreover, parcels of real estate are less homogeneous than are shares of stock, particularly shares of any one company. Then, too, real estate is far less divisible than are shares of stock. It takes surveys and new titles, all subject to governmental subdivision regulations, to divide land, whereas the stroke of a pen or a simple phone call can split a block of stock.

Real estate investments are particularly illiquid when the mortgage money "dries up." Since most real estate purchases are heavily leveraged (i.e., most are purchased largely with borrowed funds), the lack of mortgage money makes it very difficult to buy property and hence to sell it. If buyers cannot get mortgages, their willingness to buy your home is largely irrelevant; they cannot raise the money, and you probably need all of it to pay off your existing mortgage and to put a down payment on your next home (if you can find suitable financing).

Mortgage money dries up when traditional lenders, such as savings and loan associations, find better things to do with their assets than lend them long term to prospective home owners and real estate investors. The problem is sometimes caused by usury laws that forbid lenders from charging more than a certain interest rate on new mortgages. In 1979, many banks were unwilling to lend people money to buy houses because they were limited by law to 12 percent on mortgages when, at the same time, they could earn 13 percent on government bonds and over 15 percent on corporate loans. Usury laws in times of rapidly rising interest rates can cause real estate investments to be frozen for long periods of time. If sales are necessary and mortgage money is not available, owners are compelled to sell to the handful of people who are wealthy enough not to need mortgages. In such times, real estate prices tumble, and illiquidity turns into real investment losses.

Dangers in Overinvestment in Real Estate

Many people who make sound initial real estate investments subsequently ruin them with further overinvestments. *Overinvestment* refers to the making of additional capital improvements that fail to pay for themselves; in other words, the yields on these marginal investments are actually negative. In most cases, unprofitable capital improvements are based on emotional, aesthetic, and consumption motives rather than on financial considerations.

Take an example of a person who buys several low-income apartment houses, each of which is highly leveraged. Initially, the cash flow (from rents) not only covers the average variable costs, but it also covers the average fixed costs, including mortgage payments, taxes, and insurance. Shortly thereafter, the owner becomes disturbed by remarks and innuendos that the apartment houses look like slum dwellings. Determined to change that image, the owner remodels several of the apartments, plants grass and flowers around the outside, and lays new asphalt on the cratered dirt driveway. New storm windows are installed and washer-dryer attachments are set up in the basement so clotheslines full of underwear and kids' pajamas will no longer be strung across the porches.

All these improvements are tasteful, useful, and admirable, but none of them may add *significantly* to the market value of the property. Rents cannot be raised immediately usually because of leases and/or rent-control regulations. And even if rents could legally be raised, people who would be willing to pay higher rents might not be attracted to the neighborhood anyway. As a result, a profitable real estate investment becomes unprofitable.

Overinvesting in real estate is an even greater problem for home owners who suffer under the illusion that their tastes are necessarily appreciated by the market in general. This is particularly true for home improvements, such as fireplaces, swimming pools, hot tubs, saunas, and family rooms in the basement. Rarely does the addition of these investments increase the value of the house enough to make them profitable purely on a dollars and cents basis. Of course, the nonmonetary benefits might make a $10,000 hot tub that accommodates ten friends well worthwhile. To treat the tub as an investment, however, is to confuse consumption with money spent in the expectation of increasing future personal wealth.

There are investments that do add more value than their cost. The most obvious are the three P's: paint, paper, and plaster to fix up a house or to prepare it for selling. Modest kitchen remodeling and the installation of new bathroom fixtures are expenses that may be immediately recaptured in the form of a higher-than-otherwise sale price. Lavish remodeling, however, and expenditures for new appliances are costs that are seldom recovered. A new stove might cost $800, but once installed, it is no longer new, and the market for used stoves operates at far lower prices. Besides, it might not be desired by the prospective buyer who already has a stove or does not care for the type you bought.

What constitutes overinvestment as opposed to sound, positive investment in real estate depends on the particular situation. Nevertheless, it is wise to focus on resale value and on what the market wants rather than on what you want. If you plan to consume your real estate for its housing services, you can afford to make capital improvements in accordance with your preferences and your budget. On the other hand, if you are holding the real estate strictly as an investment, you cannot afford to mix your aesthetic preferences with cold, hard investment decision making. Above all, it is important not to sink more money into a real estate investment than the market price of comparable alternatives in the immediate area. Dropping $100,000 into a house located in a neighborhood full of $80,000 houses is a sure way of making a bad real estate investment—at least in the foreseeable short run.

Transactions Costs

Finally, real estate held for investment purposes has another great disadvantage, namely, the transactions costs associated with both buying and selling it. A rough figure of 10 percent of the combined purchase price and subsequent sale price is given as an estimate of these transactions costs for a round-trip investment (a single purchase and a single sale) for residential property. This figure is about 15 percent for most commercial properties. Although considerably lower than the transactions costs associated with collectibles and other tangible investments, 10 to 15 percent of the combined purchase and sale prices is not cheap. Yet these costs are often overlooked by individual investors, who can only see the purchase price and the promise of rapid appreciation ending in big capital gains.

Since the largest single transactions cost is usually the broker's fee, and since (contrary to public opinion) this fee is negotiable (at least legally negotiable), special attention should be given to reduce this disadvantage or cost of investment in real estate.

BROKERS' SERVICES AND LISTING AGREEMENTS

Most individuals do not buy or sell very many parcels of real estate during their lives. As a result, they are, for the most part, quite ignorant of the real estate market. They do not know who is looking for property (the *demand* side of the market), and they do not know who is offering comparable property (the *supply* side). Moreover, the majority of individual buyers and sellers do not understand the transfer mechanism by which real estate is passed from one person to another. Although not unfathomable, the transfer of real estate is considerably more complicated than the transfer of stocks, bonds, and other financial assets; it is also more complicated than the transfer of real assets such as gold and tangible commodities. People's lack of familiarity with the real estate market—from the standpoint of both who is trading in it and how the trades are made—provides a real need for intermediaries to bring potential buyers and sellers together. This is the reason for the existence of real estate brokers.

Typically, real estate brokers list properties of people wishing to sell. The owners are generally offered one of three types of listing agreements: an open listing, an exclusive-agency listing, and an exclusive-right-to-sell listing. In over a dozen states, listing agreements (or listing contracts) must be in writing. Even where it is not required by law, however, it is to the benefit of both the seller and the broker that the conditions of the listing agreement be spelled out and clearly understood.

An Open Listing

An *open listing* is an agreement with one or more brokers. It gives all the brokers an equal chance to "bring a meeting of the minds." The first one to do so gets the commission; the other brokers get nothing. The advantage of an open listing is that it promotes competition among brokers that can greatly benefit the seller. The disadvantage is purportedly that since no one broker has an edge, no one works especially hard to show and sell the property. There is also the disadvantage to the seller of having to deal with many brokers instead of with just one; this can be inconvenient, especially when appointments are made and broken. On the other hand, an advantage of dealing with many brokers is that the "bad ones" can be easily weeded out (by the seller's simply withdrawing the listing agreement with them); with other listing agreements, the seller might lose valuable showing time going through several brokers who are not showing the property, advertising it, or generally performing as the seller expects they should.

An Exclusive-Agency Listing

An *exclusive-agency listing* is made with one broker. It gives his or her agency the exclusive right to sell the property, *except* that the owner reserves the right to sell it directly, i.e., without any broker at all. The broker who receives an exclusive-agency listing can let other brokers work on the sale, but all offers must go through the exclusive agency's office. The selling broker gets a portion of the total commission paid to the listing broker by the owner. This portion is usually 50 to 60 percent of the total commission.

The advantage of an exclusive-agency listing is that the seller need deal (directly) only with one broker. If there is a complaint or problem, that is the broker to contact first. It is also likely that the exclusive agency will work harder to sell the property during the term of the exclusive agreement, since there is no fear that any other broker will sell it first. (Of course, the owner could still sell it directly.) From the seller's point of view, however, the term or tenure of the exclusive agency should be no more than 1 month. After that time, if the agency has not performed up to the seller's expectations, the agreement can be allowed to expire and the services of another agency can be contracted instead.

Not only should the seller be aware of the term of an exclusive-agency contract, but he or she also should remember that the commission specified in the listing agreement is negotiable until the contract is signed. In other words, it is perfectly permissible to expect that in return for giving a particular broker the edge conferred in an exclusive-agency listing, the broker will reciprocate by charging the seller a commission lower than the going rate. Unfortunately, largely out of ignorance, most sellers give exclusive listings for free or just because brokers ask for them.

An Exclusive-Right-to-Sell Listing

The third and most restrictive agreement is the *exclusive-right-to-sell listing*. This gives the broker the right to the full commission whether or not that broker actually made the sale. Regardless of whether another broker sells the property or even if the owner sells it directly, the broker holding an exclusive-right-to-sell listing is legally entitled to the full commission specified in the contract.

Again, the seller who gives a broker such a listing should be very careful of its term. Perhaps the worst mistake is to sign an exclusive-right-to-sell-until-sold agreement that virtually binds the seller to that particular broker no matter how long it takes to sell the property or how little effort the broker makes to sell it. Once the seller signs such a listing, he or she is virtually committed to paying that broker the specified commission—the only question is when.

A multiple-list arrangement is usually based on a broker's securing an exclusive right to sell. Each exclusive property listing is put with other listings in a pamphlet distributed to all the brokers who belong to the multiple-list service. If any one of these brokers sells the property, the agency holding the exclusive-right-to-sell listing automatically gets the commission, which it then divides with the selling broker. Multiple-list services are more frequently found in metropolitan areas. In rural areas, informal cobroker arrangements are made among brokers for the same purpose.

Like the exclusive-agency listing, the exclusive-right-to-sell listing is purported to give the seller the advantage of dealing with one principal broker. It is also supposed to act as an extra inducement for the listing broker to more heavily promote property for which he or she has been granted a form of monopoly power. Whether this is true or whether the seller gets better service by giving several brokers open listings depends on the particular area of the country involved. The only sure thing is that an exclusive-agency listing and especially an exclusive-right-to-sell listing have definite advantages to the brokers who make them.

BROKERS' COMMISSIONS

Although most real estate brokers profess not to "fix, control, recommend, suggest, or maintain commission rates" for their services, in fact, the rates within any one area are remarkably uniform. Typically, a 6 to 7 percent (of sale price) commission is charged for residential property and a 10 percent commission is charged for commercial and industrial property. The commission is usually billed to the seller and is collected on the date of closing or when the title is transferred. While the seller actually pays the commission, its burden falls both on the buyer and the seller because the sale price is set, in part, with the commission in mind. For example, a seller who wants $100,000 for his or her property may hope to get at least $107,500, leaving about $100,000 after the broker's 7 percent commission. (Technically, the seller would need $107,526.88 to afford a 7 percent commission and end up with exactly $100,000.) If the seller does get $107,500, he or she will, in effect, have passed the entire burden of the commission to the buyer, even though as the seller he or she actually paid the broker's commission.

From the point of view of the financial well-being of both the buyer and the seller, it is again important to recognize that brokers are third parties to most real estate sales and that their commissions are fully negotiable. This is especially true for higher-priced properties and for investment real estate in general.

Commission Negotiation by the Seller

If you are the seller, negotiation of the sales commission can begin when the property is first listed. You should contact several brokers and inquire how each of them would best approach marketing your property. Learn from them by asking specific questions:

¶ At what price should this property be listed if we hope to sell it within the next 3 months?

¶ At what price should this property sell in today's market? (This is always less than the first price quoted depending on how much "gaming" there is in the area's real estate market. In some markets, what you ask is pretty close to what you expect to get; in other markets, sellers ask more so that they have room to come down in price after negotiation with the buyer. How much listing prices are above selling prices, in general, is a measurement of how much gaming there is in the market.)

¶ How and where would you advertise this property if you were to have this listing?

¶ What extra service can you provide if I give you an exclusive-agency listing? An exclusive-right-to-sell listing?

At these initial meetings with the brokers you, the seller, should promise none of them anything. Learn from each how the game is played. Get a feel for what competition exists among the local brokers and what the differences are in the services they offer. The time you spend at this point will be well invested. The stakes are high, and even small differences in brokers' services and commissions can mean from several hundred to several thousand dollars for you.

When you do sign or verbally commit yourself to list your property, be sure that the arrangement is clear both to you and to the broker. Consider that giving several brokers an open listing may stimulate competition or it may have just the opposite effect; i.e., every broker has it so no one broker makes any special effort to sell the property. Consider limiting an exclusive-agency or an exclusive-right-to-sell agreement to a relatively short period of time (such as 2 to 4 weeks) to allow you the flexibility to change the listing arrangement. (Again, the most rigid and probably the worst arrangement is to give one broker an exclusive right to sell until the property is sold.) Consider reserving the right to sell directly to certain people who have already contacted you. Consider adding a clause that allows you to withdraw from the listing agreement on, say, a 3-day notice.

So far, all this negotiation between you (the seller) and the broker has taken place before any prospective buyers have been considered. A second time for commission negotiation can take place after the broker has found a prospective buyer but one that is unwilling to meet the price or other terms set forth in the listing arrangement. For example, you listed the property at 107,500 with a 7 percent broker commission. The broker brings you a purchase offer for $105,000. Although you may reject the offer and owe the broker nothing, you might negotiate and agree to sell the property for $105,000 if the broker would agree to a flat commission of $5000.

Negotiation for a lower broker's commission at the moment before signing the purchase offer can be an exciting, emotional event. Both you and the broker are operating at the margin. A deal worth tens of thousands (even hundreds of thousands) of dollars can be closed pending the swing of a few hundred dollars or a few thousand dollars between you and the broker. Both of you have invested time and effort building up to this moment. If you sign the purchase offer, the broker will earn a big chunk of money. If you refuse, the broker will earn nothing unless he or she can go back and persuade the prospective buyer to raise the offer price or get another buyer altogether. At the stroke of your pen, the broker could earn several thousand dollars. You agree to sign if the broker agrees to cut the commission. The tension mounts. Finally, the broker agrees to cut the commission to $5000 even. You then sign the acceptance of the purchase offer at $105,000 with a flat $5000 commission payable to the broker at the time of the actual transfer of title. In this case, your last-minute bargaining meant a saving to you of $2350, since 7 percent of the $105,000 offer would have meant a $7350 commission.

Commission Negotiation by the Buyer

If you are the buyer, you can also "negotiate" the broker's commission, even if you are not directly liable for it. Again, the time for negotiation comes at the time when you (now the buyer) have the most leverage—the moment just before you sign the purchase offer. The negotiation can take two forms. Needless to say, brokers do not like either, and most refuse to admit that they ever accept either, although they do.

The initial step is to make an offer far enough below the list price that even counteroffers and counter-counteroffers leave you and the seller apart in price. Then, after you have received the seller's "final" offer, you ask the broker to grant the seller a reduced commission so the seller will then agree to your "too low" offer. For example, suppose the seller originally wanted $107,500, you offer $100,000, the seller counteroffers with $106,000, and you counter-counteroffer with $105,000. Then you ask the broker to charge the seller a flat $5000 commission instead of the 7 percent specified in the listing agreement. If the broker agrees, the seller will end up with $100,000, i.e., the $105,000 you offer minus the $5000 broker commission paid by the seller. This is even a better deal for you, the buyer, since you pay only $105,000 instead of the seller's counteroffer of $106,000.

A second way for the buyer to negotiate the broker's commission would be to ask the broker for a cash payment. This is better known as a *kickback*. In our example, the seller's counteroffer was $106,000, and your final bid was $105,000. If the broker were willing to give you $1000 in return for your signing a purchase offer for $106,000, you would be (almost) as well off as if you and the seller had agreed on a price of $105,000. In this case, the broker would receive 7 percent on the $106,000, or $7420, minus the $1000 paid to you. Will the broker pay you a kickback? The broker's $6420 net commission is better than no sale at all, which is the stake with which you are bargaining.

Needless to say, real estate brokers do not like to be asked to give kickbacks. Offering them is often a violation of real estate regulations. Nevertheless, there is nothing illegal or immoral in your asking the broker to help you (to the tune of $1000) to purchase this property. Your only legal obligation is to report any payment to the IRS on your next income tax report. (It is reported on the front of Form 1040, where "other income" includes "side commissions, push money, kickbacks, or similar payments.") Perhaps a more subtle or palatable kickback would be one made in kind rather than in cash. For example, you might ask the broker to pay for the cost of a survey of the property, a cost that you might otherwise have to bear yourself.

FRAUDULENT LAND SALES: THE KIEFER CASE

Dick and Marge Kiefer despise the harsh winters in Plainfield, Illinois. Every March they plan a trip to either Arizona or Florida to get a week of sunshine and temperate climate. As the cost of these vacations keeps increasing, so does their desire to own vacation property in the sun belt. They figure that even a simple lot in a vacation-property area would be a good investment because of its "almost certain" appreciation and because of the income tax deductions associated with mortgage interest, property taxes, and travel to and from the lot "to inspect it" (especially in March). They would also like someday to develop their vacation property into a permanent retirement home.

Last winter Dick saw a full-page ad in a well-known magazine for lots in Arizona. He sent away for more information and was really impressed with the package of materials he received. Dreams Unlimited, a land-sales company, sent him actual photographs supposedly of lots by the beautiful Lake Bettegotcha. There were sun-bathers on sandy beaches with cool pines in the background. Maps were included with the last few lots circled by hand with a red pen. A letter explained that these lots were not the "last of the litter," but were actually among the first choices of other smart investors who had been "forced" to cancel their purchases because of a death in the family or some other unforeseen circumstance. Dick was advised to hurry before these last, choice pieces were sold to a long list of other eager investors. The package also contained letters from supposedly satisfied investors who had already purchased these fabulous lots. They reiterated all the advantages of such real investments, which promised not only financial rewards but years of consumption benefits as well.

To further assure the Kiefers, Dreams Unlimited sent them a copy of the professional opinion of a CPA (certified public accountant) and the legal opinion of an attorney who was "a specialist in vacation-land sales." The Kiefers also were invited to their local Holiday Inn on a selected date for a free roast beef dinner. Moreover, if they signed a purchase offer at that time, they were to receive ten "big" silver dollars. If financing would be a problem, the Kiefers were guaranteed a mortgage to be easily paid off at only $50 per month. "For this price, how could they go wrong?" There was no mention of the annual percentage rate, the finance charge, or how long these easy $50 monthly payments were to go on.

Dick was excited and ready to go to the Holiday Inn, have a nice roast beef dinner, lay $1000 down on lot 235 near the end of Lake Bettegotcha, and begin to make plans for his little recreation-vacation-retirement Lincoln-Log-style home. However, that evening he and Marge saw a report on television about land sales in Florida. It showed how thousands of people had been cheated by flimflam land-fraud schemes. The report said that there were no state laws governing land sales and that the federal government only got involved when more than 300 lots were being sold by one developer with annual sales in excess of $500,000.

The TV report further cautioned against being snookered by free gifts, free meals, and free trips—none of which are really free if you have to subject yourself to an intensive sales pitch before receiving the free goods. Furthermore, it advised prospective investors to

¶ Comparison shop among alternative properties in other locations.
¶ Review the purchase offer contract with a competent attorney before signing it.
¶ Never waive the right to cancel your offer within 3 business days.
¶ Not buy before carefully examining the property in person.

Dick and Marge went to the "free" roast beef dinner, but they were intent on being cautious. They listened to the developer's spiel, and they watched the rest of a well-rehearsed sound and light show extolling the virtues of an investment in property on Lake Bettegotcha. They were tempted to follow other investors who actually rushed forward after the final slide show to grab a lot. Instead, they asked if they could go to Arizona the following week specifically to see lot 235. They were told (firmly) that all the lots would be sold by then. The Kiefers left without signing, without the ten silver dollars, but with the haunting feeling that they had just passed up the deal of a lifetime.

A month later Marge saw a letter to the editor in the local newspaper from a couple who had gone to see their lot on Lake Bettegotcha. They said that the so-called development was in a flat desert area and that the lake was not yet flooded. If and when it ever would be, the average depth was expected to be only 2 feet. Presently, there were no roads, no utilities, and no signs of any development except for hundreds of wooden markers with little pieces of red tape on them. When this couple had tried to get their money back, the Arizona Attorney General had informed them that the developer had gone bankrupt and had left the state; there was nothing he could (or would) do for them.

Marge breathed a sigh of relief. From now on she was determined to carefully analyze any real estate investments the family might consider. She would be exceptionally careful of anyone who claimed, "You can't lose by investing in land."

CALCULATION OF A REAL ESTATE
INVESTMENT'S RATE OF RETURN

Most people do not have the ability to compute the rate of return on even a relatively simple investment in real estate. The reasons are very similar to those which make computation of the rate of return on cash-value life insurance so difficult. First, there are many different expenditures and often many different receipts generated by a real estate investment, and some of these have significant tax consequences. (By analogy, with cash-value life insurance, over a 20-year period you will have many premiums to pay, many dividends to receive, and cash value accumulated on a tax-deferred basis.) Second, the timing of these real estate expenditures and receipts cannot be ignored. Just as the net-cost analysis of a life insurance policy is an unacceptable and false method of measuring its cost, so too is simply subtracting dollar outlays and receipts on a real estate investment, particularly one that took place over a period of several years. An example from the lives of Dick and Marge Kiefer illustrates these problems.

Seven years ago Dick bought a small piece of land (25 by 100 feet) on Route 52 not far from Plainfield. He paid $3000 for the property plus $200 for lawyer's fees and other transfer costs. Taxes on this land have remained at $100 each year.

Five years ago he built a small billboard out of used telephone poles and scrap steel purchased at the local junk yard. The total cost of the billboard was $2600. Since then he has rented the space to a restaurant that pays him $500 each year. (The billboard is red with white letters; it says, "Eat at Uncle Luigi's!")

Last month a realtor appraised the property at $10,000 and asked Dick if he would list it. The commission on such so-called commercial property is customarily 10 percent. Marge asked Dick to assume he would sell the property for $10,000 and to compute the rate of return on his investment. Their daughter, Sheila, said that was easy. She whipped out her new TI Whiz Kid calculator, divided the $10,000 sale price by $3000 purchase price and proclaimed that her dad had made 333 percent rate of return on his investment.

Dick set out a bit more methodically and based his calculations on the information given in Table 7.1. Dick

Table 7.1   Information to Calculate the Rate of Return on the Kiefers' Real Estate Investment Over 7 Years

	(−)	(+)
Purchase price	$3000	
Purchase transactions cost	200	
Cost of billboard (5 years ago)	2600	
Rents from billboard ($500 per year × 5 years)		$ 2500
Taxes paid ($100 per year at end of each year)	700	
Sale price (assumed)		10,000
Sale transactions cost (broker, lawyer, other fees)	1200	
	$7700	$12,500

treated his original investment as the sum of the purchase price plus the purchase transactions cost. Based on this investment of $3200, he calculated the net rate of return as follows (refer to Chapter 1 for an explanation of this formula):

$$IN (1 + r)^n = OUT$$
$$(3000 + 200)(1 + r)^7 = -2600 + 2500$$
$$- 700 + 10{,}000 - 1200$$
$$3200(1 + r)^7 = 8000$$
$$r = 13.99 \text{ percent per year}$$

Dick figured that his $3200 investment grew to $8000 (with a net dollar return of $4800) in 7 years. This represents a 150 percent increase or a compound annual rate of return of 13.99 percent per year.

Marge was not happy. She said that Sheila's figure was completely wrong and that Sheila should think before cranking numbers into her Whiz Kid calculator. She also told Dick that his simple rate of return was too simple. It was like their life insurance salesman's net-cost method that "proved" they would pay nothing for their life insurance and even get money back. She knew there was something wrong; the payments and receipts came at different times and had to be discounted or expanded to reflect a common point in time. If Dick had learned nothing else from their analysis of life insurance (Chapter 6), he should have known better than to add or subtract raw numbers from different points in time. Dick knew Marge was right but said jokingly, "My estimate is close enough for government work."

Marge took Sheila's calculator and some statistical tables she found at the back of *Consumer Economics,* a book she had used in college. She chose (rather arbitrarily) the 8 percent tables to discount (annually) for time and inflation over the past 7 years. Like a life insurance expert (as opposed to a typical life insurance salesperson), she decided to expand all the past data to today's values. (Her accumulated-value technique is identical to the interest-adjusted cost method described in the previous chapter.) She expanded the $3000 purchase price of 7 years ago to $5141 today, since $1 left for 7 years would grow to $1.7138 according to her 8 percent tables (refer to Table 7.2). She did the same for the purchase transactions cost and adjusted it from $200 to $343. The $2600 cost of the billboard was multiplied by 1.08^5, or 1.4693, to adjust its value to $3820. The $500 in annual rents were adjusted by a factor of 6.3359 to yield $3168. The $100 in annual taxes were adjusted by a factor of 8.923 to $892. The sale price and sales transactions cost did not require time adjustment because they would be received or paid today. Finally, she was ready to compute the annual rate of return as follows:

$$(5141 + 343)(1 + r)^7 = -3820 + 3168 - 892 + 10{,}000 - 1200$$

$$5484(1 + r)^7 = 7256$$

$$(1 + r)^7 = 1.3231$$

$$r = 4.08 \text{ percent per year}$$

243

**Table 7.2   The Kiefers' Real Estate Investment Data
with Values Accumulated to Today**

	(−)	(+)
Purchase price ($3000 × 1.7138)	$ 5141	
Purchase transactions cost (200 × 1.7138)	343	
Cost of billboard (5 years ago) ($2600 × 1.4693)	3820	
Rents from billboard ($500 per year, at the beginning of each of last 5 years) ($500 × 6.3359)		$ 3168
Taxes paid (100 per year at end of each of 7 years)	892	
Sale price (estimated)		10,000
Sale transactions cost (broker, lawyer, other fees)	1200	
	$11,396	$13,168

Marge figured that the original investment plus transactions cost was $5484 ($5141 + 343) and that it grew to $7256 with a net real-dollar return of only $1772. This represents a 32 percent increase or a compound annual dollar return of only 4.08 percent.

Intent on proving that Dick's real rate of return was indeed only 4.08 percent per year, Marge recalculated the investment based on values 7 years ago. Instead of expanding past values to current ones, she discounted current ones back to those of 7 years ago. Her data were transformed into the numbers shown in Table 7.3. She

**Table 7.3   The Kiefers' Real Estate Investment Data
with Values Discounted to 7 Years Ago**

	(−)	(+)
Purchase price	$3000	
Purchase transactions cost	200	
Cost of billboard (2 years after original purchase)	2229	
Rents from billboard ($500 per year, at the beginning of each of last 5 years) ($500 × 3.6970)		$1849
Taxes paid ($100 per year at end of each of 7 years)	521	
Sale price (estimated) ($10,000 × 0.5835)		5835
Sale transactions cost (broker, lawyer, other fees) ($1200 × 0.5835)	700	
	$3950	$7684

computed the net return's value as of 7 years ago as

$$(3000 + 200)(1 + r)^7 = -2229 + 1849 - 521 + 5835 - 700$$
$$3200(1 + r)^7 = 4234$$
$$(1 + r)^7 = 1.3231$$
$$r = 4.08 \text{ percent per year}$$

This calculation, on an investment whose cost 7 years ago was $3200, also gives an interest-adjusted or real rate of return of 32 percent or a compound annual rate of return of 4.08 percent. This real rate of return is exactly the same as that computed in terms of today's values. This is as it should be, since it makes no difference what point in time is chosen, as long as all the data are adjusted to that particular point.

Marge's calculations are indeed more accurate, although both she and Dick forgot several factors that are unique to real estate as an investment. First, while they included the value of the property taxes paid each year ($100) as a cost, they failed to include the benefit of that expense as an income tax deduction. If they are in the 35 percent tax bracket, this $100 per year property tax deduction saved them $35 at the end of each year when they paid their taxes. This is a positive "return" on their investment and should not be ignored.

Second, a more serious omission was their neglect of income taxes on the annual rents. They counted $500 at the beginning of each year as a positive return but did not acknowledge that 35 percent of this amount (or $175) disappeared for income taxes at the end of each year.

Likewise, they failed to see that their capital gain for income tax purposes was $3000. Their capital gain is the adjusted sale price ($8800) minus the adjusted purchase price ($3200) minus capital improvements ($2600). This "gain" will be taxed currently as ordinary income. Since they are in the 35 percent tax bracket, this would mean a capital gains tax (as part of their income tax) of $1050. Of course their capital expense (the $2600 billboard) could have been depreciated, which would have resulted in greater annual tax savings (with a rise in capital gains taxes at the end of the investment).

Obviously, the income tax considerations involving property taxes, interest on a mortgage (not a factor in the Kiefer example), capital gains taxes, and depreciation are very important and must be included in a careful analysis of the rate of return on a real estate investment. They can (and should) be estimated, time-adjusted, and included on the right side of our rate-of-return formula. (Marge knew this, but she had already successfully deflated Dick and his estimate of a return of 13.99 percent per year.)

When Dick saw his psychiatrist that week, he complained of Marge's "deflating his investment ego." He was feeling put down. His daughter Sheila had thought he was brilliant with a 333 percent rate of return. Even he thought he was pretty smart with a return of 13.99 percent per year. But he could not argue with Marge's computation of a real rate of return of only 4.08 percent per year. The psychiatrist, who dropped out of business school to become an analyst, scratched numbers on a small piece of paper. Finally, he said, "You really should have more self-esteem, Richard. Had your wife used a 4 percent discount factor, your real rate of return would have been 8.9 percent per year, which is not bad compared to alternative investments, at least those available to middle-income people like yourself." Dick felt better in spite of paying his analyst $75 for the half hour on the couch. Was the analyst's estimate correct? (*Answer:* Yes, although it also neglected tax considerations and 4 percent is an unrealistically low time rate of discount. Marge was closer.)

POINTS TO REMEMBER

¶ It is often difficult to assess the advantages and disadvantages of a real estate investment, in part because there are often important nonmonetary considerations, such as the desire to own something tangible or the fear of being trapped with an illiquid asset.

¶ Expected benefits and costs associated with real estate investments are difficult to assess, since they may rely heavily on your future tax bracket. They are subject to radical effects caused by changes in income and property tax laws, interest ceilings, rent controls, and zoning regulations.

¶ The most serious shortcoming in evaluating real estate investments is the failure to reckon benefits and costs (or receipts and outlays) at a common point in time.

¶ Discounting or expanding benefits and costs is an exercise that is vital to an accurate estimate of the investment's real rate of return.

¶ Failure to adjust benefits and costs to one point in time causes wide variations in the assessment of the overall value of the investment.

8

PORTFOLIO MONITORING
AND MANAGEMENT

If you wish to compute the annual rate of return r on one particular investment whose value in the past was V_o and whose value today is V_1, you must solve the following formula, where t represents the number of years between the two valuations:

$$V_o(1 + r)^t = V_1$$

In other words, the value of the investment in the past (V_o) multiplied by 1 plus the annual rate of growth ($1 + r$) raised to the number of years between the two valuations (t) is equal to the value today (V_1). By now this should be very familiar; we have seen this formula, or variations of it, used in every chapter in this book. (In Chapter 1 we called it $IN(1 + r)^n = OUT$.) *If* no additions to or withdrawals from a personal wealth portfolio are made, the formula is easily adapted to measure the overall annual rate of return between any two points in time. Thus you may compute the annual rate of return on your personal wealth between what it was 18 months ago (W_o) and what it is today (W_1) by solving the formula for r:

$$W_o(1 + r)^{18/12} = W_1$$

In this case, your wealth 18 months ago (W_o) multiplied by 1 plus the annual rate of growth ($1 + r$) raised to the $18/12$ power is equal to your wealth today (W_1).

Unfortunately, the requirements that there be no additions to or withdrawals from the portfolio are not usually met. New investment money is often added to one's portfolio from earnings or from outside sources, such as gifts and inheritances. Likewise, interest, dividends, and other unearned income may be taken from the portfolio and used for current consumption or given to someone else. If this is the case, simply measuring the value of the portfolio at two points in time, plugging these values into the formula, and solving for r is meaningless at best and quite often seriously misleading. A simple example will explain why.

Suppose that I tell you that last year I had an investment portfolio consisting of 200 shares of XYZ stock, 50 LMN bonds, and $30,000 in a money market mutual fund and that the portfolio's total value was $100,000. If I also tell you that my investment portfolio now consists of 100 shares of RST stock, 20 OPQ bonds, and $85,000 in a money market mutual fund and that the portfolio's total value is now $110,000, you only could conclude that I made 10 percent on my investments *if* you assumed that no outside money was added to the portfolio and none was taken from the portfolio. The fact that the portfolio grew in size is no promise of a positive rate of return on its investments unless these conditions are met. The portfolio might have grown simply because of an addition to it from my savings or from some other outside source.

Most investment portfolios do receive infusions of outside money and do make distributions to outside consumption over the course of a year or more. Thus our simple formula for computing a rate of return between any two points in time is usually not valid. What is valid is to treat an investment portfolio as a mutual fund and to compare the growth of its net asset value between the desired two points in time.

With any mutual fund, the *net asset value per share* (*NAV*) is simply the total value of all its assets minus its debts, all divided by the number of shares it has issued. Where there are no debts,

$$\frac{\text{Total value of assets}}{\text{Number of shares}} = NAV \qquad \text{or}$$

$$\text{Total value of assets} = \text{number of shares} \times NAV$$

What this means is that once the number of shares is decided on, the net asset value per share is simply the total value divided by the number of shares.

As we saw in Chapter 5, mutual funds set the number of shares initially so that their *NAV* is typically between $10 and $30. There is no good reason for doing this, other than that this is the price range for many common stocks with which investors may be better acquainted. A mutual fund that issued a larger number of shares such that its *NAV* was, say, $1 per share might appear to be more speculative to investors who mistakenly compare it with low-priced or "penny" stocks. On the other hand, if the same mutual fund issued a very small number of shares such that its *NAV* was, say, $200 per share, investors might regard it as being somehow "overpriced" with less chance for appreciation. However, as we have seen before, the expected rate of growth of a mutual fund is in no way indicated by its current *NAV,* which is determined largely by the number of shares that the fund has chosen to issue. Indeed, a fund's *NAV* can rise or fall precipitously with no change in its total value or its growth potential. It makes no difference if an investor has 1000 shares of a fund with an *NAV* of $20 or 2000 shares of a fund with an *NAV* of $10. In either case, the investment is worth $20,000.

Likewise, an individual can initialize his or her wealth portfolio at any *NAV* by simply arbitrarily setting the number of shares such that when the total asset value is divided by this number it will produce the desired *NAV.* A simple example will illustrate how to initialize an individual's portfolio to begin to treat it as a mutual fund.

INITIALIZING AN INDIVIDUAL PORTFOLIO

Suppose that J. J. Jones had personal wealth consisting of two assets: $8000 in a money market mutual fund and $12,000 in 400 shares of ABC stock currently selling at $30 per share. This $20,000 portfolio could initially be treated as a mutual fund with 2000 JJJ shares with an *NAV* of $10 per share. The number of shares, 2000, was chosen arbitrarily. However, once it has been chosen, the *NAV* is determined by dividing the $20,000 total asset value by the number of shares. In this case, once the initial number of JJJ shares was set at 2000, the *NAV* became $20,000/2000, or $10 per share:

Money market mutual fund (MMMF) shares	8000
Price per share	$ 1
Current value of MMMF	$ 8000
ABC stock (ABC) shares	400
Price per share	$ 30
Current value of ABC stock	$12,000
Total JJJ portfolio value	$20,000
Number of JJJ shares	2000
Net asset value of the JJJ portfolio (*NAV*)	$ 10

Once Jones's individual portfolio is "initialized," we can begin to talk about the number of JJJ shares and the *NAV* of the JJJ portfolio. Let's explore how each of several events could change the size of the JJJ portfolio and its *NAV*. Later we shall trace this portfolio and see how it changes over a number of periods.

BUYING WITH NO COMMISSION

When money from outside the portfolio is used to buy into or expand the portfolio, its impact depends on whether or not there are commissions or other significant transactions costs. If Jones takes $3100 from his savings (not considered a part of the JJJ portfolio) and invests this money in his money market mutual fund, he is buying into the JJJ portfolio with no commission. It would be like buying 310 JJJ shares at $10 per share. The total JJJ portfolio value would increase to $23,100, and the number of JJJ shares would increase to 2310. The *NAV* would remain at $10 per share. The portfolio would look like this:

	Initial Portfolio	After a $3100 Buy with No Commission
Money market mutual fund (MMMF) shares	8000	11,100
Price per share	$ 1	$ 1
Current value of MMMF	$ 8000	$11,100
ABC stock (ABC) shares	400	400
Price per share	$ 30	$ 30
Current value of ABC stock	$12,000	$12,000
Total JJJ portfolio value	$20,000	$23,100
Number of JJJ shares	2000	2310
Net asset value of the JJJ portfolio (*NAV*)	$ 10	$ 10

BUYING WITH A COMMISSION

If $3100 is brought into the portfolio and is used to buy something with a commission, part of the portfolio is eaten away and its *NAV* declines. In our example, suppose the $3100 from savings is brought into the money market mutual fund and Jones then writes a check for

$3100 to buy 100 shares of ABC, including a $100 broker's commission. When the $3100 was brought into the portfolio, the number of JJJ shares increased to 2310. When the additional 100 shares of ABC was purchased, the number of JJJ shares remained the same; nothing left the JJJ portfolio at this point; $3100 of the money market mutual fund was simply traded for $3000 of ABC stock, with $100 being eaten up in commissions. This caused the total value of the JJJ portfolio to fall from $23,100 to $23,000 and hence the *NAV* fell to 9.957. Notice that the *NAV* fell even as the portfolio expanded in size. Notice also that even if the outside money ($3100) were used to buy the additional 100 shares of ABC directly (as opposed to going first into the money market mutual fund), the results would have been the same. (However, if the additional 100 shares of ABC had come as a gift, the *NAV* would have remained at $10 because there would have been no commission, at least not for Mr. Jones. Rather, there would have been a simple $3000 in extra value brought into the portfolio in the form of 100 shares of ABC stock.)

	Initial Portfolio	After a $3100 Buy with a $100 Commission
Money market mutual fund (MMMF) shares	8000	8000
Price per share	$ 1	$ 1
Current value of MMMF	$ 8000	$ 8000

	Initial Portfolio	After a $3100 Buy with a $100 Commission
ABC stock (ABC) shares	400	500
Price per share	$ 30	$ 30
Current value of ABC stock	$12,000	$15,000
Total JJJ portfolio value	$20,000	$23,000
Number of JJJ shares	2000	2310
Net asset value of the JJJ portfolio (*NAV*)	$ 10	$ 9.957

SELLING WITH NO COMMISSION

If part of the portfolio is sold, its total value will always decline, but its *NAV* will only decline if there were significant transactions costs. (The adjective *significant* refers to sizable brokers' commissions, fees, and special taxes. *Insignificant* transactions costs would include postage or phone costs associated with making a transaction.) If a check is written on Jones's money market mutual fund for $5800 to pay for his daughter's tuition, the initial portfolio would change like this:

	Initial Portfolio	After a $5800 Sale with No Commission
Money market mutual fund (MMMF) shares	8000	2200
Price per share	$ 1	$ 1
Current value of MMMF	$ 8000	$ 2200

	Initial Portfolio	After a $5800 Sale with No Commission
ABC stock (ABC) shares	400	400
Price per share	$ 30	$ 30
Current value of ABC stock	$12,000	$14,200
Total JJJ portfolio value	$20,000	$14,200
Number of JJJ shares	2000	1420
Net asset value of the JJJ portfolio (*NAV*)	$ 10	$ 10

Writing this check is the same as selling 580 shares of the JJJ portfolio with no transactions costs. Such a sale leaves the *NAV* unchanged, even though Jones's wealth fell from $20,000 to $14,200.

SELLING WITH A COMMISSION

Trading assets within the portfolio will not change the number of JJJ shares. It will lower the *NAV,* however, if there are significant transactions costs. If Jones sells 200 shares of ABC for $6000 minus a $200 commission and puts the net proceeds from the sale ($5800) into his money market mutual fund, the number of JJJ shares will remain at 2000, but his *NAV* will fall to $9.90. If he then writes a check for $5800 to pay the tuition bill, the *NAV* remains at $9.90, but his number of JJJ shares drops to 1414.141. His new portfolio would look like this:

	Initial Portfolio	After a $5800 Net Sale with a $200 Commission
Money market mutual fund (MMMF) shares	8000	8000
Price per share	$ 1	$ 1
Current value of MMMF	$ 8000	$ 8000
ABC stock (ABC) shares	400	200
Price per share	$ 30	$ 30
Current value of ABC stock	$12,000	$ 6000
Total JJJ portfolio value	$20,000	$14,000
Number of JJJ shares	2000	1414.141
Net asset value of the JJJ portfolio (*NAV*)	$ 10	$ 9.900

EXPERIENCING A SHARE DIVIDEND

Many assets yield returns in the form of additional shares. For example, the shares in a typical money market mutual fund increase at the end of every day. In a money market mutual fund growing at 10 percent, 10,000 shares at $1 per share today will become $[1 + (0.10/365)] \times 10,000$ or 10,002.74 shares tomorrow and $[1 + (0.10/365)] \times 10,002.74$ or 10,005.48 shares the next day and 10,008.221 shares the day after. The impact of these share dividends on an individual portfolio is to increase its total value and its *NAV*. In the case of the JJJ portfolio, if its money market mutual fund grew at 10 percent for 30 days (with no change in the ABC stock), the portfolio would look like this:

	Initial Portfolio	After 30 Days, MMMF Share Dividend
Money market mutual fund (MMMF) shares	8000	8066.015
Price per share	$ 1	$ 1
Current value of MMMF	$ 8000	$ 8066.02
ABC stock (ABC) shares	400	400
Price per share	$ 30	$ 30
Current value of ABC stock	$12,000	$12,000
Total JJJ portfolio value	$20,000	$20,066.02
Number of JJJ shares	2000	2000
Net asset value of the JJJ portfolio (*NAV*)	$ 10	$ 10.0330

Likewise, if Mr. Jones's ABC stock paid a share dividend of 2 shares for every 100 he holds, or if it paid warrants (rights to buy additional shares at a fixed price on or before a certain date), his portfolio's value would increase and so would its *NAV*. The same is true for interest on bonds, mortgages, or certificates of deposit; as the interest accumulates, both the portfolio's total value and its *NAV* increase.

There is one notable exception to the impact of a typical share dividend, and that is in the case of a mutual fund distribution in the form of additional shares, i.e., a distribution of the interest, dividends, and capital gains earned on its investments. Remember, the *NAV* of any mutual fund already includes the interest, dividends, and capital gains accumulated from its investments in stocks, bonds, etc. Thus, when a mutual fund (other than a money market mutual fund, whose *NAV* is held constant at $1) distributes its earnings in the form of additional shares, its *NAV* drops proportionately. Its total value is the same before and after the share distribution; the fund simply increased its number of shares and hence caused its *NAV* to drop proportionately. Unlike a share distribution (in lieu of cash dividends) on a stock investment, a share distribution on a typical mutual fund (other than a money market mutual fund) is no cause for celebration, because the value of your investment remains exactly the same. Since this distinction is very important, let us illustrate it with an example.

If a (stock) mutual fund, such as the 44 Wall Street Fund, declares a 50 percent dividend distribution, and if you previously owned 600 shares worth $12 per share, immediately after the distribution you would have 900 shares worth $8 per share. However, you have no net gain; both before and after the distribution you owned $7200 worth of the 44 Wall Street Fund. Do not confuse share dividends for stocks and share distributions (of dividends, interest, and capital gains) for mutual funds.

EXPERIENCING A CASH DIVIDEND

When stock dividends, bond interest, or money market mutual fund dividends are received in cash (actually in the form of a check as opposed to cold, hard, green cash), part of what the portfolio is generating is being removed from it. If nothing else changes, the total value of the portfolio remains constant; its number of shares decreases and its *NAV* increases.

To see this more clearly, set up a cash account within the portfolio. As dividend checks are received, put them into this account. Notice that the total value and the *NAV* increase. Then withdraw the cash or take it out and consume it; this is equivalent to selling off a portion of your portfolio. Notice that the portfolio's total value drops to its initial level, but the *NAV* remains the same. Overall total value is the same as it was initially, but the *NAV* has risen.

In our example, if Mr. Jones receives a (monthly) check from his money market mutual fund for $66, and if he does not reinvest it in his portfolio, his *NAV* increases to 10.033 while his number of JJJ shares drops to 1993.422:

	Initial Portfolio	$66 MMMF Cash Distribution	$66 Cash Removed
Money market mutual fund (MMMF) shares	8000	8000	8000
Price per share	$ 1	$ 1	$ 1
Current value of MMMF	$ 8000	$ 8000	$ 8000
ABC stock (ABC) shares	400	400	400
Price per share	$ 30	$ 30	$ 30
Current value of ABC stock	$12,000	$12,000	$12,000
Cash account	$ 0	$ 66	$ 0

	Initial Portfolio	$66 MMMF Cash Distribution	$66 Cash Removed
Total JJJ portfolio value	$20,000	$20,066	$20,000
Number of JJJ shares	2000	2000	1993.422
Net asset value of the JJJ portfolio (*NAV*)	$ 10	$ 10.033	$ 10.033

However, this scenario is not the case for cash distributions from typical (non-money market) mutual funds. If mutual fund distributions of interest, dividends, and capital gains are received in a check, the situation is different. In this case, the *NAV* remains constant, but both the total value and the number of shares in the portfolio decline. This is because these mutual fund distributions do not benefit your portfolio; the remaining mutual fund value drops by an amount equal to that which has been distributed in cash. Thus your portfolio's *NAV* remains constant. When you do not reinvest the amount distributed in cash, both the total value and the number of shares in your portfolio decline.

THE NULL TRANSACTION

If you simply want to check the status of the portfolio as of a certain date, you may run what is called the *null transaction*. In this case, there are no buys, no sales, and no changes in the portfolio other than changes in the prices of each asset. In our example, if the price of ABC stock falls to $28 per share, and if there are no other changes in the portfolio, our null-transaction calculation would show the *NAV* to fall from $10 to $9.60:

	Initial Portfolio	Null Transaction
Money market mutual fund (MMMF) shares	8000	8000
Price per share	$ 1	$ 1
Current value of MMMF	$ 8000	$ 8000
ABC stock (ABC) shares	400	400
Price per share	$ 30	$ 28
Current value of ABC stock	$12,000	$11,200
Total JJJ portfolio value	$20,000	$19,200
Number of JJJ shares	2000	2000
Net asset value of the JJJ portfolio (*NAV*)	$ 10	$ 9.60

CALCULATING THE PORTFOLIO'S RATE OF RETURN

The buys, sells, and cash distributions occurring in most portfolios preclude computing their annual rates of return with the formula

$$W_o(1 + r)^t = W_1$$

Nevertheless, we can treat any portfolio as a mutual fund (and specifically one that never makes share or cash distributions) and solve for *r* using the formula

$$NAV_o(1 + r)^t = NAV_1$$

Therefore, if the JJJ portfolio had an *NAV* last year of $10 and an *NAV* this year of $11.50, we could say that its annual rate of growth was 15 percent. If this change had occurred over a 6-month period (that is, $t = \frac{1}{2}$ instead of $t = 1$), then the compound annualized rate of return or rate of growth of the portfolio would have been 32.25 percent.

Now you can see the primary reason for setting up your portfolio as a mutual fund. Between any two points in time, a simple comparison of the *NAV*s reveals the rate of growth over that period. Although you cannot compare *NAV*s to compute the rate of growth of a typical mutual fund (unless you are sure that the fund has not made any distributions of interest, dividends, and capital gains), you can compare *NAV*s for your personal portfolio because there are never any share or cash distributions from the portfolio, only buys and sells. (Of course, there can be share and cash distributions from assets *within* the portfolio, but there are no arbitrary distributions whereby your personal portfolio's *NAV* is lowered and its number of shares raised proportionately.)

Let's make this distinction crystal clear. If you were told that the 44 Wall Street Mutual Fund had an *NAV* last year of $8 and an *NAV* today of $10, you could not conclude that the fund grew 25 percent *unless* you knew for sure that it had made no distributions of its interest, dividends, or capital gains. Conversely, if you knew there had been no such distributions, you could conclude it had grown 25 percent, that is,

$$\$8(1 + r)^1 = \$10$$

$$r = 25 \text{ percent}$$

From your personal portfolio, there are never any distributions of interest, dividends, and capital gains, so comparisons of *NAV*s are valid for computing rates of growth. Let's turn now to a comprehensive example showing how a hypothetical personal portfolio changes over several periods of time.

A COMPREHENSIVE MULTI-PERIOD EXAMPLE

Suppose we start the JJJ portfolio, as we did earlier, with just two assets: $8000 in a money market mutual fund and 400 shares of ABC stock evaluated at $30 per share. Again, we can arbitrarily "initialize" this JJJ portfolio with 2000 shares, giving the portfolio a net asset value (*NAV*) of $10 per share.

At time period 1 (which we might assume comes right after initialization), Mr. Jones invests $10,000 in this portfolio by buying 10,000 additional shares of the money market mutual fund, each share of which is worth the constant amount of $1. With no share dividends or price changes, his portfolio's total value would increase to $30,000 with 3000 shares and the same *NAV* of $10 per share:

	Initial Portfolio	**1** Buy $10,000 of MMMF with No Commission	**2** Buy 100 Shares ABC Stock with $100 Commission
MMMF shares	8000	18,000	18,000
Price per share	$ 1	$ 1	$ 1
Value of MMMF	$ 8000	$18,000	$18,000
ABC stock shares	400	400	500
Price per share	$ 30	$ 30	$ 30
Value of ABC stock	$12,000	$12,000	$15,000
JJJ portfolio value	$20,000	$30,000	$33,000
JJJ shares	2000	3000	3310
NAV	$ 10	$ 10	$ 9.9698

At time period 2, Mr. Jones takes $3100 of outside money and buys 100 more shares of ABC and pays a $100 commission. With no share dividends or price changes, this $3100 investment buys an additional 310 JJJ shares. However, because of the commission, the portfolio's total value increases by only $3000 to $33,000. As a result, dividing $33,000 by 3310 shares gives us a new and lower *NAV* of $9.9698.

At time period 3, Mr. Jones decides to sell $3000 worth of his money market mutual fund. (Perhaps he writes a $3000 check on his money market mutual fund to pay off a home-improvement loan.) Since there is no commission, the *NAV* remains at $9.9698, but his total number of JJJ shares drops to 3009.09. To pay off the loan, he effectively sold 300.91 shares worth $9.9698 each for a total of $3000. (*Note:* The numbers might not add exactly due to rounding, but this is not a problem for individual portfolio analysis. It is wise, however, to carry decimals, at least those for *NAV,* out to four places.)

	3 Sell $3000 of MMMF with No Commission	4 Sell 300 Shares ABC; Proceeds to MMMF; $200 Commission	5 Remove Net Proceeds from Previous Sale
MMMF shares	15,000	23,800	15,000
Price per share	$ 1	$ 1	$ 1
Value of MMMF	$15,000	$23,800	$15,000
ABC stock shares	500	200	200
Price per share	$ 30	$ 30	$ 30
Value of ABC stock	$15,000	$ 6000	$ 6000
JJJ portfolio value	$30,000	$29,800	$21,000
JJJ shares	3009.09	3009.09	2120.50
NAV	$ 9.9698	$ 9.9033	$ 9.9033

At time period 4, Mr. Jones sells 300 shares of ABC stock at $30 per share and pays a $200 commission. He puts the net proceeds $8800 (i.e., 300 shares times $30 per share minus $200 in commissions) into his money market mutual fund. These transactions occur within the portfolio. He sells one asset and buys another; no outside money is involved. Therefore, the number of JJJ shares remains unchanged at 3009.09. The transactions are not frictionless, however, and $200 of the JJJ total value is eaten up in commissions. The new and lower total value of $29,800 divided by the same number of JJJ shares (3009.09) shows a decline in the *NAV* to $9.9033.

At time period 5, Mr. Jones removes the net proceeds ($8800) from the money market mutual fund and takes them outside the portfolio. This is like a sale with no commission. The *NAV* remains at $9.9033. It is equivalent to Mr. Jones selling 888.59 shares of the JJJ portfolio, each share being worth $9.9033, and taking the proceeds ($8800) outside.

Comparing the events of periods 1 to 5 teaches us that our primary concern is not the size of the portfolio, but the rate of change in its net asset value. Outside money coming into the portfolio increases its size, but it tells us nothing about how well the portfolio is managed. This is indicated by how fast the *NAV* increases. Likewise, funds leaving the portfolio to pay outside expenses are no reason to depreciate the portfolio's performance. However, commissions paid when rearranging the portfolio or when buying or selling a portion of it are a cause for concern; by itself, paying commissions always causes a drop in *NAV*.

At time period 6, Mr. Jones makes no transaction. He simply wants to check on the status of his portfolio. Since the last period, the price of ABC stock has increased from $30 to $40 per share. The null transaction shows that the total value of his portfolio has risen to

$23,000. Since the number of JJJ shares remains unchanged (at 2120.50), the *NAV* has risen to $10.8465:

	6 Null Transaction; Price of ABC Goes Up	7 Null Transaction; Price of ABC Goes Down	8 $200 MMMF Dividend Kept in the MMMF
MMMF shares	15,000	15,000	15,200
Price per share	$ 1	$ 1	$ 1
Value of MMMF	$15,000	$15,000	$15,200
ABC stock shares	200	200	200
Price per share	$ 40	$ 35	$ 35
Value of ABC stock	$ 8000	$ 7000	$ 7000
JJJ portfolio value	$23,000	$22,000	$22,200
JJJ shares	2120.50	2120.50	2120.50
NAV	$ 10.8465	$ 10.3749	$ 10.4692

At time period 7, another null transaction is run. Here the only change from the previous period is that the price of ABC stock has fallen from $40 to $35 per share. As a result, the total value of the JJJ portfolio has fallen to $22,000. Since the number of JJJ shares remains unchanged (at 2120.50), the *NAV* has fallen to $10.3749.

At time period 8, a $200 share dividend is reported for Mr. Jones's money market mutual fund. We know that most money market mutual funds pay and record share dividends at the end of every day. However, there is no need to update an individual portfolio this often. It is wise, however, to update a money market mutual fund account periodically, *and it is necessary to update before the portfolio is altered by any new buys, sells, or dividends*. A simple phone call will give you the most recent balance on a money market mutual fund. The portfolio can be brought up to date to include all recent interest accrued on the account in the form of additional shares (each valued at $1). By itself, this will increase the portfolio's *NAV*. Then, based on the most recent total value and the *NAV*, the impact of new buys, sells, or dividends may be calculated.

At time period 9, the ABC stock pays a cash dividend of $2.50 per share, or $500. Mr. Jones decides not to keep this money in his portfolio, but instead to use the $500 for outside expenses. Were this cash dividend on ABC stock kept in the portfolio, the portfolio's total value would have risen to $22,700. With 2120.50 JJJ shares, the *NAV* would have risen to $10.7050. However, the $500 dividend was not kept in the portfolio, so its total value remains at $22,200 with a *NAV* of $10.7050. Dividing total value by the new and higher *NAV* ($22,200/$10.7050) gives us the remaining number of JJJ shares, 2073.79. The stock dividend was a plus for the JJJ portfolio; it caused its *NAV* to increase. The fact that Mr. Jones decided not to keep the $500 dividend in the portfolio is equivalent to his selling off a part of it. Hence the number of JJJ shares falls from 2120.50 to 2073.79:

	9 $500 ABC Dividend Taken in Cash	10 $300 MMMF Dividend Plus ABC Price Change	11 2-for-1 ABC Stock Split
MMMF shares	15,200	15,500	15,500
Price per share	$ 1	$ 1	$ 1
Value of MMMF	$15,200	$15,500	$15,500
ABC stock shares	200	200	400
Price per share	$ 35	$ 40	$ 20
Value of ABC stock	$ 7000	$ 8000	$ 8000
JJJ portfolio value	$22,200	$23,500	$23,500
JJJ shares	2073.79	2073.79	2073.79
NAV	$ 10.7050	$ 11.3319	$ 11.3319

At time period 10, two events occur, both of which serve to increase the *NAV* of Mr. Jones's portfolio. First, $300 in accrued dividends on the money market mutual fund are added. This is treated as a share dividend. Second, the price of ABC stock rises from $35 to $40 per share. As a result of both these events, the portfolio's total value rises to $23,500. With the same number of shares, this causes the *NAV* to rise from $10.7050 to $11.3319.

At time period 11, there is a two-for-one stock split for ABC. Notice that Mr. Jones now has twice as many shares of ABC but that each share is worth only half as much as it was just prior to the split. Consequently, there

271

is no change in the size, the number of shares, or the *NAV* of the JJJ portfolio.

At time period 12, Mr. Jones decides to purchase six LMN bonds with outside money recently inherited from his grandmother. Each bond costs $950. All six bonds cost $5700, plus $60 in commissions, for a total cost of $5760. If Mr. Jones had brought the $5760 into his portfolio in a new cash account or into his money market mutual fund, his total portfolio value would have been $29,260. The $5760 divided by the *NAV* just before he brought the $5760 in ($11.3319) would have been equivalent to buying 508.2996 additional shares of the JJJ portfolio for a total of 2582.09 shares.

In purchasing the bonds, $60 was eaten up in commissions, so Mr. Jones's total portfolio value is now only $29,200. This number divided by the new number of JJJ shares (2582.09) gives us his new and lower *NAV* of $11.3087:

	12 Buy 6 LMN, $60 Commission, Outside Money	**13** Buy 4 LMN, $40 Commission, Inside Money	**14** Buy $10,000 ZZZ Fund, No Load
MMMF shares	15,500	11,660	1660
Price per share	$ 1	$ 1	$ 1
Value of MMMF	$15,500	$11,660	$ 1660
ABC stock shares	400	400	400
Price per share	$ 20	$ 20	$ 20
Value of ABC stock	$ 8000	$ 8000	$ 8000

272

	12 Buy 6 LMN, $60 Commission, Outside Money	13 Buy 4 LMN, $40 Commission, Inside Money	14 Buy $10,000 ZZZ Fund, No Load
LMN bonds	6	10	10
Price per bond	$ 950	$ 950	$ 950
Value of LMN bonds	$ 5700	$ 9500	$ 9500
ZZZ Fund shares			833.333
Price per share			12
Value of ZZZ shares			$10,000
JJJ portfolio value	$29,200	$29,160	$29,160
JJJ shares	2582.09	2582.09	2582.09
NAV	$ 11.3087	$ 11.2932	$ 11.2932

At time period 13, four LMN bonds are purchased with inside money taken from the money market mutual fund. The bonds cost $950 each, for a total of $3800, plus a $40 commission. Therefore, $3840 is withdrawn from the money market mutual fund (probably by check) to pay for the four bonds worth $3800. The portfolio is simply being rearranged; there is no change in its number of JJJ shares. When its new total value ($29,160) is divided by the same number of shares (2582.09), the NAV falls to $11.2932. Had there been no commissions, the transfer would have left total value and NAV unchanged as well. This is illustrated in time period 14.

273

Here we see $10,000 worth of the money market mutual fund being transformed into $10,000 worth of the ZZZ (no-load) Mutual Fund. Since there are no commissions to sell the money market mutual fund shares and no commissions to buy the ZZZ Mutual Fund shares, there is no loss in the total value or in the *NAV* of the portfolio.

At time period 15, the LMN bonds each pay $50 in interest. If Mr. Jones kept this money ($500) in his portfolio, its total value would have risen to $29,660. This total value divided by the previous number of JJJ shares (2582.09) gives him the higher *NAV* of $11.4868. However, keeping the interest in cash outside the portfolio is like selling part of the portfolio. The number of shares falls to 2538.56.

At time period 16, Mr. Jones records the impact of changing prices by running a null transaction. The price of his ABC stock falls, but the prices of both his bonds and his ZZZ Mutual Fund shares rise. Overall, the total value of his portfolio (with 2538.56 JJJ shares) rises to $29,443.33 and its *NAV* rises to $11.5984:

	15 $50 per Bond Interest in Cash	16 Null Transaction, Price Changes	17 1.5-for-1 Share Distribution, ZZZ Fund
MMMF shares	1660	1660	1660
Price per share	$ 1	$ 1	$ 1
Value of MMMF	$ 1660	$ 1660	$ 1660

274

	15 $50 per Bond Interest in Cash	16 Null Transaction, Price Changes	17 1.5-for-1 Share Distribution, ZZZ Fund
ABC stock shares	400	400	400
Price per share	$ 20	$ 18	$ 18
Value of ABC stock	$ 8000	$ 7200	$ 7200
LMN bonds	10	10	10
Price per bond	$ 950	$ 975	$ 975
Value of LMN bonds	$ 9500	$ 9750	$ 9750
ZZZ Fund shares	833.333	833.333	1250
Price per share	$ 12	$ 13	$ 8.67
Value of ZZZ shares	$10,000	$10,833.33	$18,833.33
JJJ portfolio value	$29,160	$29,443.33	$29,443.33
JJJ shares	2538.56	2538.56	2538.56
NAV	$ 11.4868	$ 11.5984	$ 11.5984

At time period 17, the ZZZ Fund distributes its accrued interest, dividends, and capital gains. Mr. Jones takes a portion in the form of additional shares, namely, 1.5 new shares for each old share. Notice that this share distribution is not like a dividend on a stock or interest on a bond. Although the number of ZZZ shares rose by 50 percent, the value per share fell proportionately, leaving no net gain in the value of Mr. Jones's ZZZ holdings. Consequently, the total value, the number of shares, and the *NAV* of the JJJ portfolio all remain the same.

At time period 18, Mr. Jones again runs the null transaction to see the effect an increase in the price of the ZZZ Mutual Fund from $8.67 per share to $9.00 per share. The total value of his portfolio rose to $29,860, and with the same number of JJJ portfolio shares, the *NAV* rose to $11.7626.

At time period 19, the accrued share dividend of Mr. Jones's money market mutual fund ($240) was accounted for along with increases in the prices of his ABC stock and his ZZZ Mutual Fund. Since there were no buys or sells, there was no change in the number of JJJ shares. The total value of the portfolio rose to $32,150, and consequently, the *NAV* rose to $12.6646:

	18 Null Transaction, Price Changes	19 $240 MMMF Dividend Kept in Plus Price Changes	20 $1000 Cash Distribution, ZZZ Fund
MMMF shares	1660	1900	1900
Price per share	$ 1	$ 1	$ 1
Value of MMMF	$ 1660	$ 1900	$ 1900
ABC stock shares	400	400	400
Price per share	$ 18	$ 20	$ 20
Value of ABC stock	$ 7200	$ 8000	$ 8000
LMN bonds	10	10	10
Price per bond	$ 975	$ 975	$ 975
Value of LMN bonds	$ 9750	$ 9750	$ 9750

	18 Null Transaction, Price Changes	19 $240 MMMF Dividend Kept in Plus Price Changes	20 $1000 Cash Distribution, ZZZ Fund
ZZZ Fund shares	1250	1250	1250
Price per share	$ 9	$ 10	$ 9.20
Value of ZZZ shares	$11,250	$12,500	$11,500
JJJ portfolio value	$29,860	$32,150	$31,150
JJJ shares	2538.56	2538.56	2459.60
NAV	$ 11.7626	$ 12.6646	$ 12.6646

Finally, at time period 20, the ZZZ Mutual Fund makes a distribution of its interest, dividends, and capital gains in the form of a check that Mr. Jones spends (instead of reinvesting in his portfolio). The amount of this distribution is $1000. Notice that the value of Mr. Jones's 1250 shares of the ZZZ Mutual Fund fall by exactly $1000, the same amount as the distribution. The total value of the portfolio falls by $1000, and the NAV remains the same. The number of JJJ shares falls from 2538.56 to 2459.60, which is equivalent to the sale of exactly $1000 worth of the JJJ portfolio. (The difference between 2538.56 and 2459.60 is 78.96 JJJ shares, which when multiplied by the NAV of $12.6646 is exactly equal to the $1000 in cash distributions taken out of the portfolio.)

PORTFOLIO ANALYSIS

Maintaining your portfolio, as Mr. Jones did in the preceding example, offers distinct advantages. As we have already shown, you can easily compute the overall rate of return between any two points in time by employing the formula

$$NAV_o(1 + r)^t = NAV_1$$

For example, if 21 months had passed between initialization and time period 21, we could compute the rate of return on Mr. Jones's portfolio over the entire period as follows:

$$\$10(1 + r)^{21/12} = \$12.6646$$

$$r = 14.45 \text{ percent per year}$$

We might also analyze the performance over shorter time periods. For example, consider the 6 months between time periods 12 and 18. Here the *NAV* rose from $11.3087 to $11.5984, or

$$\$11.3087(1 + r)^{6/12} = \$11.5984$$

Solving, we might conclude that $r = 5.19$ percent per year. However, caution must be exercised in drawing such conclusions for short periods of time unless all aspects of the portfolio have been considered. Notice that between time periods 12 and 18 no updating of the money market mutual fund was performed, yet we know that share dividends were accrued and added daily to

Mr. Jones's money market mutual fund balance. Nor were stock dividends, which might have been declared but not yet paid, reckoned in computing the *NAV*s between these two periods. Our comparative analysis of *NAV*s is only as good as the degree to which all aspects of the portfolio are considered. Over longer periods, accrued interest, dividends, etc. are more likely to be acknowledged; hence longer-period comparisons are usually more valid than those made for shorter periods.

REFINEMENTS

For most people, monitoring a personal portfolio, as we have demonstrated, is a complicated but rewarding task. It allows you to review your portfolio at a glance and to make relatively simple computations of gains and losses. For those who wish to refine this approach, here are a few amendments.

Deferred Availability

A *deferred-availability asset* can be added to include money that is owed to you or that will become available in the future. For example, on June 1, the ABC Corporation may declare a $2 per share dividend to all shareholders as of July 15 to be paid August 15. If you hold 400 shares on July 15, you can expect $800 in dividends on August 15:

	July 14: Updated Portfolio	July 15: $2 per Share Dividend Declared for ABC	August 15: $800 Dividend Received and Put in MMMF
MMMF shares	1900	1900	2700
Price per share	$ 1	$ 1	$ 1
Value of MMMF	$ 1900	$ 1900	$ 2700
ABC stock shares	400	400	400
Price per share	$ 20	$ 20	$ 20
Value of ABC stock	$ 8000	$ 8000	$ 8000
LMN bonds	10	10	10
Price per bond	$ 975	$ 975	$ 975
Value of LMN bonds	$ 9750	$ 9750	$ 9750
ZZZ Fund shares	1250	1250	1250
Price per share	$ 9.20	$ 9.20	$ 9.20
Value of ZZZ shares	$11,500	$11,500	$11,500
Deferred availability		800	
Price per share		$ 1	
Value of deferred availability		$ 800	
JJJ portfolio value	$31,150	$31,950	$31,950
JJJ shares	2459.60	2459.60	2459.60
NAV	$ 12.6646	$ 12.9899	$ 12.9899

On July 15, you enter a "share dividend" of 800 shares at $1 per share of "deferred availability." This causes your portfolio's total value to rise and its *NAV* to rise. Then on August 15, when you actually receive the $800 check and put it into your money market mutual funds, you sell 800 shares of your deferred-availability asset and buy 800 shares of your money market mutual fund. With no transactions costs, your portfolio's total value, number of shares, and *NAV* all stay the same. (On the other hand, if you kept the $800 dividend check outside your portfolio and consumed it, you would "sell" 800 shares of your deferred availability on August 15; this would cause the total value of your portfolio and its number of shares to decline, but there would be no change in the *NAV.*) A deferred-availability account is a handy way of recording and keeping track of money you expect but do not yet have in your possession.

Deferred Liability

A *deferred-liability asset* can be handled in the same fashion as a deferred-availability one, except that the price of $1 per share is always negative. Suppose that you sold all of your ZZZ Mutual Fund shares. If you received $11,500 and had originally paid $10,000, you would have made a capital gain of $1500. If you are in the 28 percent marginal tax bracket (and if there are no capital gains exclusions), you will owe the government income taxes of 0.28 times $1500, or $420. This $420 liability could be recorded in your portfolio by taking a "share dividend" of 420 shares of a deferred liability evaluated at minus $1 per share:

	Sept. 1: Updated Portfolio	Sept. 1: Sold All Shares of ZZZ No-Load Fund	April 15: $420 Tax Liability Paid with Check on MMMF
MMMF shares	2700	14,200	13,780
Price per share	$ 1	$ 1	$ 1
Value of MMMF	$ 2700	$14,200	$13,780
ABC stock shares	400	400	400
Price per share	$ 20	$ 20	$ 20
Value of ABC stock	$ 8000	$ 8000	$ 8000
LMN bonds	10	10	10
Price per bond	$ 975	$ 975	$ 975
Value of LMN bonds	$ 9750	$ 9750	$ 9750
ZZZ Fund shares	1250	0	0
Price per share	$ 9.20	$ 9.20	$ 9.20
Value of ZZZ shares	$11,500	$ 0	$ 0
Deferred liability		420	0
Price per share		$ −1	$ −1
Value of deferred availability		$ −420	$ 0
JJJ portfolio value	$31,950	$31,530	$31,530
JJJ shares	2459.60	2459.60	2459.60
NAV	$ 12.9899	$ 12.8192	$ 12.8192

As a result of the tax liability, the total value of your portfolio would decline; the number of shares would stay the same and the *NAV* would fall. When you actually pay the taxes (and hence eliminate the liability) with a check drawn on your money market mutual fund, the event would be treated as a sale of 420 shares of your money market mutual fund and the sale of the deferred liability. If there were no price changes, dividends, interest, etc., the total value of the portfolio would remain unchanged, as would the number of shares and its *NAV*.

Debts

For longer-term liabilities, a *debt entry* can easily be included in a personal portfolio. If you borrow, say, $10,000 to buy 500 more shares of ABC, you would buy 500 more shares of ABC and you would buy 10,000 units of debt priced at *minus* $1 per unit. If there were no transactions costs, the net effect would be to leave the total value of your portfolio, its number of shares, and its *NAV* all unchanged (if there were transactions costs associated with borrowing, total value and *NAV* would decline):

	Updated Portfolio	Borrow $10,000 to Buy 500 ABC, No Commissions	Repay $5000 of the Debt with Funds Taken From the MMMF
MMMF shares	13,780	13,780	8780
Price per share	$ 1	$ 1	$ 1
Value of MMMF	$13,780	$ 13,780	$ 8870
ABC stock shares	400	900	900
Price per share	$ 20	$ 20	$ 20
Value of ABC stock	$ 8000	$ 18,000	$ 18,000

	Updated Portfolio	Borrow $10,000 to Buy 500 ABC, No Commissions	Repay $5000 of the Debt with Funds Taken From the MMMF
LMN bonds	10	10	10
Price per bond	$ 975	$ 975	$ 975
Value of LMN bonds	$ 9750	$ 9750	$ 9750
Debt units		10,000	5000
Price per unit		$ − 1	$ − 1
Value of debt		$ − 10,000	$ − 5000
JJJ portfolio value	$31,530	$ 31,530	$ 31,530
JJJ shares	2459.60	2459.60	2459.60
NAV	$ 12.8192	$ 12.8192	$ 12.8192

As interest owed accrues on your debt, it is treated like a share dividend. It can be updated periodically with an increase in the number of units of the debt. Thus, in the case of a 10 percent $10,000 debt, after 1 year it would be treated as 11,000 units of a debt priced at minus $1 per unit. This means that each time interest owed is increased, there is a fall in the total value of the portfolio and a fall in *NAV*, but there is no change in the number of portfolio shares.

When the debt, or a portion of it, is paid off from within the portfolio, the transaction is treated as the sale of, say, 5000 money market mutual fund shares and the sale of 5000 units of the debt. These sales, taken together, leave the total portfolio value, the number of shares, and the *NAV* all unchanged.

POINTS TO REMEMBER

¶ If, between two points in time, money is added to or subtracted from a portfolio of assets, the annual rate of return on that portfolio cannot be computed by simply comparing the size of the portfolio at those two points.

¶ If a personal portfolio is treated as a mutual fund that makes no share or cash distributions, then its rate of growth can be easily computed from its net asset values (per share) at any two points in time.

¶ Buying into or selling part of the portfolio does not change its *NAV* *unless* there are transactions costs, in which case *NAV* will fall.

¶ Share dividends on stock, warrants, and interest accumulated on bonds and other debt instruments all cause a portfolio's total value and *NAV* to increase.

¶ Distributions by mutual funds (of accrued interest, dividends, and capital gains) in the form of extra shares or in cash leave a portfolio's total value, number of shares, and *NAV* all unchanged.

¶ Cash dividends represent a removal of assets from a personal portfolio, unless they are put back in as a cash asset. Cash dividends cause the portfolio's *NAV* to increase.

¶ Cash dividends should not be confused with cash distributions from a mutual fund (other than a money market mutual fund), which do not cause the personal portfolio's *NAV* to rise.

¶ A deferred-availability asset in a personal portfolio is used to record money that is expected in the near future but which is not yet in your possession.

¶ A deferred-liability asset has a negative price and reflects money, now in your portfolio, that you will owe in the near future.

¶ Deferred liabilities might be generated by taxes to be paid as the result of assets you sold with capital gains. They also might be generated by assets you purchased but for which you have not yet paid.

¶ Longer-term liabilities may be put in a category called "debts." Interest accrued on these debts is treated as share dividends with a negative price. Payment of the debt is treated as a sale.

ENDNOTES

CHAPTER 1

1. The illiquidity associated with real estate can be alleviated by establishing a line of credit based on the equity in the property. Home equity loans allow a portion of the equity or ownership in the real estate to be liquidated or turned into money. Nevertheless, real estate is considered to be an illiquid asset because usually it cannot be sold at its fair market value quickly and easily.

2. One investment service recommends that the earnings-to-price (E/P) ratio (the reciprocal of the P/E ratio) be at least twice as high as the yield on an AAA bond. In other words, if the yield on an AAA bond is 8 percent, a stock should not be considered unless its E/P ratio is at least 16 percent; i.e., unless its P/E ratio is no more than 6.25.

3. See Gerald Appel, *Winning Stock Selection Systems* (New York: Boardroom Reports, 1979), and Norman G. Fosback, *Stock Market Logic: A Sophisticated Approach to Profits on Wall Street* (Ft. Lauderdale, Fla.: Institute Econometric, 1976).

CHAPTER 2

1. *Earned income* comes from labor, usually in the form of wages and salaries. *Unearned income* includes dividends, interest, capital gains, rents, and other nonlabor income.

2. A *debit card* allows you to transfer funds from your bank account directly into the accounts of certain merchants who also have accounts with your bank or correspondent institutions.

3. Focus on these three attributes: (1) short term, (2) high grade, and (3) IOU. Then see how each of these money market assets has all three attributes. Federal government debt in the form of Treasury bills or in the form of Treasury notes or Treasury bonds that will mature, say, within 3 months. Bank debt (insured by the FDIC) issued in the form of certificates of deposit that will mature soon. A corporation check, say, for $10,000, that has been dated 2 months from now and that has been guaranteed "accepted" by the bank on which it is written. (The bank has accepted the check, meaning it has agreed to pay it 2 months from now. The acceptance makes the bank, not just the corporation, responsible to whomever holds the check.) Lastly, consider an IOU of a large, well-established corporation, such as IBM, that is due 1 month from now. This would be considered commercial paper and, again, constitutes a short-term, high-grade IOU.

4. This example is presented in Richard L. D. Morse, *Check Your Interest* (Manhattan, Kansas: Morse Publications, 1979), p. 3.

CHAPTER 4

1. Many investors buy bonds that are expected to depreciate in market value as they approach maturity. Such bonds are bought "at a premium." But the investors believe the value of their higher expected interest income will outweigh this expected capital depreciation.

CHAPTER 6

1. In 1979, a student at Hobart and William Smith Colleges learned that every president elected in a year ending in zero died while in office. The student tried to buy a $100,000 life insurance policy on President Carter's life, naming the Colleges as the beneficiary. The request was denied because the student did not have an insurable interest in the president's life; it was merely a gamble

to raise money for his old alma mater. (The Secret Service did not think much of the idea either.)

2. See *Cost Facts on Life Insurance,* published by the National Underwriter Company (420 E. Fourth Street, Cincinnati, Ohio 45202), or a comparable compilation. To be sure that you are dealing with a sound, well-managed company, you should ask for a copy of *Best's Report and Rating* or look up the company in *Best's Insurance Reports,* available in the library. You also might be well advised to read the three-part series "Life Insurance," published by *Consumer Reports* (June, July, August 1986) or *Life Insurance: How to Buy the Right Policy from the Right Company at the Right Price,* published by *Consumer Reports Books.* This book can be obtained by ordering Code 151, and sending a check for $12 (plus $3 postage and handling = $15) to: Consumer Reports Books, P.O. Box 589, Stratford, CT 06497-9984.

SELECTED REFERENCES

Ansbacher, Max G. *The New Options Market.* New York: Walker Publishing Co., 1987.

Consumers Union. "Life Insurance" (a three-part series). *Consumer Reports,* June, July, August 1986.

Darst, David M. *The Complete Bond Book.* New York: McGraw-Hill, 1975.

Engel, Louis. *How to Buy Stocks,* 6th Ed. New York: Bantam Books, 1977. (Most stock brokers can give you a copy of this book for free.)

Malkiel, Burton G. *A Random Walk Down Wall Street.* New York: Norton, 1985.

Merrill Lynch, Inc. *What Is Margin?* (a 24-page pamphlet available from Merrill Lynch, One Liberty Plaza, 165 Broadway, New York, NY 10080).

"Original Issue Deep Discount Bonds." *Federal Reserve Bank of New York Quarterly Review,* Winter 1981–1982, pp. 18–28.

Sherwood, Hugh C. *How to Invest in Bonds.* New York: McGraw-Hill, 1983.

"What You Should Know about Discount Stock Brokers." *Consumer Reports,* October 1976, pp. 588–591.

Index

ABOUT THE AUTHOR

photo: Neil Sjoblom

Daniel McGowan describes himself as a white-collar worker with blue-collar interests. Since 1973 he has been a Professor of Economics at Hobart and William Smith Colleges where he teaches courses in personal finance, monetary theory, and consumer economics. He is a licensed real estate broker and a financial planner. He is frequently asked to appear in court as a forensic economist to testify in cases involving death, disability, and dissolutions of marriage or job contracts. He has written several textbooks on economics and is a lifetime member of Consumers Union and the National Rifle Association. He and his wife and their twin daughters live in Geneva, New York.